SPECIAL OCCASIONS IN EMBROIDERY

TO MAKE AND TREASURE

JILL CARTER

B. T. Batsford Ltd
London

Dedication

For MODBM

Acknowledgements

Firstly I thank my children and family who have put up with a long period of 'organised chaos' and helped whenever possible.

I have much appreciated the loyal support of my friends. With special thanks to Ann Carter, Sarah Nichols and Sarah Deem for completing all that I threw at them in record time with humour and considerable skill. Also to Valerie Campbell-Harding for her infectious enthusiasm, generous support and encouragement. I would also like to thank Jean Pike, Jan Sugden, Barbara Slade, Ruby Lever, Jane Corin, Joanna Philpot, Barbara Yorke-Edwards, Linda Gould and Brigid Peat. All have unfailingly spared me their precious time and effort to work samples and projects and their assistance has brought another dimension to creating this book.

I would like to thank the team at Batsford for their hard work – Venetia Penfold, my editor, and DWN's designers, Paul Tavener and Vicky Harvey, who have all turned my manuscript into a beautiful book. Finally I thank my dear friend, Ann Bartleet, who has quietly and constantly been supportive of all I have done.

I gratefully acknowledge the generous contributions of materials, fabrics and equipment from Peter Armatage, Appleton Brothers; Jill Devon, The Bead Merchant; Clive Beardall, Antique Furniture Restoration; Eddie and Rose Wiffen, The Cheap Shop; Alistair McMinn, Coats Craft UK; Cara Ackerman, DMC Creative World; Stef Francis; Ginny Barnston, Ginny's Heirlooms; David Pritchard, CMP Habico; John Lewis Partnership; Rosemary Lowery, Lowery Workstands; Marilyn Becker, Ribbon Designs; Kathy and Arthur Warner, Village Fabrics; William Weil, George Weil and Sons.

First published in paperback in 2001
B T Batsford 9 Blenhein Court
Brewery Road
London N7 9NT

A member of the Chrysalis Group plc

A catalogue record for this book is available from the British Library.

ISBN 0 7134 8637 6

Printed and bound by The Bath Press, Bath

Photography by Marie-Louise Avery
Copy edited by Vivienne Wells
Line illustrations by Anthony Lawrence
Author portrait on jacket by Geoff Meadowcroft

Publishers' Acknowledgements

The publishers would like to thank the following for generously lending props for photography:

Sue Leaver, 3 Church Hill Cottages, Leavenheath, Essex for making a Christmas cake; Missy Graves and Graham Hughes, Tatters, 74 Fulham Road, London SW3 6HH for the loan of one of their designer wedding dresses; Eric French, Bulbanks Farm, Aldham, Essex for a Christmas tree (out of season!); Annabel Lewis, V V Rouleaux, 10 Symons Street, London SW3 2TJ for decorative ribbons; Sally Scobie, Nippers, Whites Farm, Bures Road, White Colne, Colchester, Essex CO6 2QF for a baby's cot; Jason Waterworth, Nice Irma's, 46 Goodge Street, London W1P 1FJ for vases. In addition, thank you to Fiona and Jack Crase who modelled the Welcome Shawl with such professionalism.

Note: the black arrows on the charts indicate the centre lines.

CONTENTS

INTRODUCTION

The dictionary definition of Heirloom is 'a piece of valuable personal property which descends to the Heir-at-law, by special custom'. For me, that is only part of the story. The value of inheriting or being given an embroidered heirloom has also to do with the subliminal meaning hidden or symbolised in the design, the creation of the embroidery itself, the reason for the work and, of course, the embroiderer. The pleasure of working and giving such an embroidery is matched only by receiving it and is intensely personal. I have lasting examples of beautiful embroidery, lovingly worked by my mother, grandmother, great aunt Mollie and great, great aunts Ella and Dora, all of which I treasure and enjoy.

The projects in this book will take you through many of the important milestones in life, with the chance to celebrate each occasion with an embroidery that will last as an heirloom for future generations to cherish.

The book is divided into four main sections: Weddings, New Arrivals, Special Occasions, and Christmas, with titles to reflect the nature of the embroidery, and also the hidden messages within flower names. Some of the projects are traditionally accepted heirlooms using a contemporary approach, such as the delicate Christening Gown and Welcome Shawl, the Triptych Wedding Sampler in Cross Stitch, and the Drawn Thread Sampler worked in Hardanger embroidery. I have also introduced different ideas such as the Kneeler Cushions, a Christening Cracker, small decorative hangings and the Cake Band. Each chapter draws you into a series of projects which allow you to explore and combine your artistic skills, but most importantly are for you to enjoy. Whether you are new to embroidery or an experienced needleworker, you will find something to inspire you and to express your own creative message.

Six different embroidery techniques have been used: Canvas work, Cross stitch, Hardanger embroidery, Heirloom sewing, Quilting and Surface embroidery. Listed materials, clear instructions, designs and charts show you how to work each project.

The introductory chapters give comprehensive information and materials, working techniques and clear stitch illustrations. These will help you to undertake anything you decide to try in the book. Alternative ideas and variations are suggested to inspire you further.

The joy of embroidery is that it has a place for us all. This book has been prepared in the hope that it will provide a portrait of colours, skills, love and devotion, coupled with the patience and perseverance which are necessary for life itself.

Jill Carter

Jill Carter 1997

hugo

CHAPTER 1

MATERIALS AND TECHNIQUES

In this chapter you will find instructions and step-by-step diagrams for all the basic techniques used in the book, including embroidery stitch techniques. Read the relevant section to familiarize yourself with the information before tackling any of the projects.

Traditional threads and fabrics have been used but you can always explore the possibilities of using more unusual threads. If you like to paint or dye, try dyeing your own threads and fabric where appropriate.

MADE IN
ENGLAND

CANVAS WORK

Stitching on canvas is currently one of the most popular forms of embroidery, as it is not only a satisfying and relaxing hobby, but also a stimulating form of creative expression. Throughout history, canvas work has reflected contemporary trends in design and fashion. Rekindled interest in embroidery on canvas has established it as a practical craft for fashion and for the home – appropriate for items as wide-ranging as fire-screens, bed and wall-hangings, carpets, slippers, bags, cushions, chair seats, pincushions and numerous other smaller items. The wealth of wonderful threads now available encourages stitchers to try exciting new effects and gives them the opportunity to incorporate other embroidery techniques not usually associated with canvas work.

Canvas

Since you are going to take precious time and trouble stitching these projects, it makes sense to use a good-quality canvas. There are a number of different types of canvas on the market, but for most projects I prefer a polished mono de-luxe (single-thread) canvas. Canvas is available in white and shades of ecru (antique), and comes in different sizes of mesh (number of threads to the inch).

I have indicated the colour and size for each project (the right colour prevents the background from showing through if your stitches are not absolutely perfect). If you use a finer or coarser canvas than the one given, your finished work will be smaller or larger (respectively) than the given size.

Threads

Organize and label your threads so that you know which shade you are using. There are many thread organisers now on the market – choose one to suit your needs and enjoy the simple pleasure of having the thread for your project neatly stored and all together! Make sure you have bought enough yarn from the same dye lot to complete your piece.

Woollen yarns: The projects are worked using Appleton crewel wool and the correct number of strands for each stitch is given in the instructions. If you decide to work with Paterna (Paternayan) Persian or DMC Medici yarns you will have to make small allowances for differences in thickness and colour (see page 142 for conversion chart).

It is best to cut hanks of Appleton crewel wool into three equal lengths (long lengths of yarn wear thin before they are finished). Shape the hank into a circle and cut through the hank at 12 o'clock. Take hold of the ends at the right-hand side of the cut and pull down through the middle to 6 o'clock. Adjust the yarn so that you have three equal lengths and then cut top and bottom as shown (Fig. 1). Turn the outside-right length top to bottom so

that all the yarn is twisting in the same direction. Then tie the threads together about 5cm (2in) from one end and consistently take the thread from that end into the needle.
If the yarn becomes twisted as you stitch, let your needle hang freely to untwist the thread, or run the needle up and down the thread.

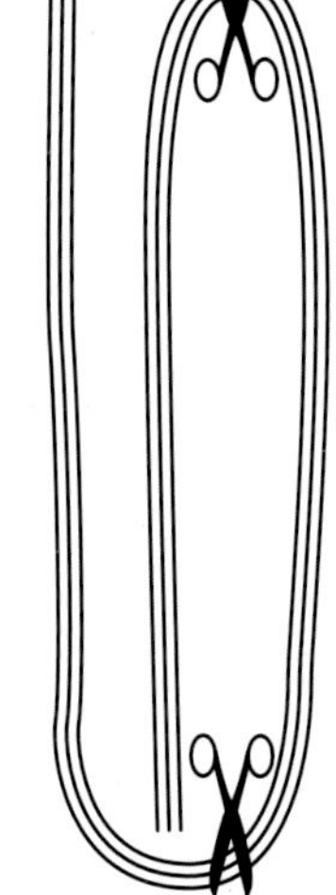

Fig. 1

Stranded cotton (floss): I have used Anchor stranded cotton (floss). Always 'strip' the cotton before you use it. That is, pull each of the six strands apart, placing them flat side by side. Put the required number back together, lightly moisten your finger and thumb and run them down the thread. This will make the cotton lie smoothly on the canvas and give better coverage.

Silk or satin ribbon: Handle and position ribbon with care so that it does not twist, but lies as flat as possible on the surface of the canvas. It helps to slip the ribbon over your finger or a laying tool such as a large needle as you sew.

Always use a blunt-ended tapestry needle. The size of the needle depends on the size of the canvas mesh. The project instructions give details of the correct needle for each project.

Frames

I strongly recommend the use of a frame, as this encourages a more even stitch tension and reduces distortion of the canvas. Using a frame also makes it easier to see where you are going. For the projects in this book you will need a hand-held or floor standing roller frame, or a square wooden frame or artist's canvas stretcher bars.

Mounting work on a roller frame

Always allow at least 5cm (2in) of unworked canvas round the design and, if it is necessary to mark the canvas in any way, use a waterproof marker; never a lead pencil (the lead could 'bleed' on to your work when it is dampened for stretching).

To stabilize and neaten the edges, machine or hand stitch white cotton tape to all four sides of the canvas, having removed the selvage. Find the centre of the canvas by folding it loosely into quarters and gently creasing the centre point. Mark the centre lines with a line of tacking (basting) stitches and match with the centre point on your roller frame. Use the herringbone pattern on the frame's webbing as a guide line to keep the canvas straight. Working from the centre outwards, first pin one half of the canvas onto the webbing and oversew in place. Repeat on the second half and then the opposite side.

Once you have assembled the frame, roll up the work tightly and lace the sides into position using a strong string. Leaving long ends, pass the string through the taped sides of canvas, over the side bars and back down through the canvas at 25mm (1in) intervals. Tighten and adjust the strings equally either side, then wrap and tie the long tails round the ends of the bars to secure. Untie and adjust these strings when unrolling the canvas to work on a different area of the design.

Mounting work on artist's canvas stretcher bars

To construct a square with the bars, ease the corners together and firmly interlock. Sometimes sandpaper is needed to smooth off rough edges. Position the wooden pegs that come with the bars to give a right-angled corner. Centre the canvas over the bars, ensuring that the canvas is straight and the warp and weft are lying parallel to the bars. Use drawing pins or a staple gun to secure the canvas to the bars, keeping it taut and firm. Fold the edges of canvas over the bars to the back and cover with masking tape to prevent snagging. If necessary, trim away excess canvas.

Starting and Finishing

To keep your work uniform and neat, use one of the following methods:

Waste-knot method

Start with a knot at the end of your thread on the surface of the work, about 2cm (¾in) from your first stitch. Work towards the knot, so that the thread is firmly secured at the back of the fabric by your stitches. When you reach the knot, cut it carefully, close to the canvas.

Away-knot method

This is best for separate motifs, or when you might be able to see the thread running behind light stitches or pulled-thread work. Start with a waste knot about 10cm (4in) away from where you are working. When the motif is complete, cut the knot, re-thread the tail of thread and weave it securely through the back of the stitching.

Weaving method

This is mostly used when an area is crowded with stitchery and you need to start a new thread to complete a small area. Weave the new thread through the back of previous stitches and fix with one or two small back stitches.

Finishing a thread

Bring your thread to the surface, about 2cm (¾in) away from the stitching, horizontally or vertically. Leave the thread hanging on the front of the fabric. Introduce a new thread and continue stitching. When the old thread is covered, trim off its tail level with the canvas and continue stitching as before. Alternatively, weave the thread carefully through the back of the work. This method can lead to 'mole-hills' on the front of the work, particularly with tent stitch and should be used as little as possible.

Starting and finishing a ribbon

Ribbon has to be treated differently, as it is not sufficient to weave in the ends. Start with an away knot, but, when working in the ribbon or finishing off, it must be firmly anchored to the back of previous stitches using small back stitches and sewing thread. The starting and finishing ends of the ribbon may be stitched to each other when working a single motif.

Keeping your work clean

Store your canvas work carefully in a protective bag or pillow case to keep it clean. If you are working with pastel colours it is a good idea to cover completed areas with a clean handkerchief, cloth or tissue paper to prevent any dirty marks as you stitch.

Blocking / stretching canvas

Once you have finished your stitching (even if you have worked on a frame), you will need to block/stretch the canvas to set the stitches, straighten out any minor distortion of the canvas and make the work look more even and professional. You may prefer to use a professional stretching service, but if you wish to try your own stretching, I hope that the following instructions will be helpful.

1 Use a thick board, larger than your canvas, but of wood soft enough to take drawing pins or rust-proof tacks.

2 Cover the board with old sheeting (to prevent snags and staining from the wood), stretched tightly and secured in place with drawing pins or staples.

3 Draw a grid of guide lines at 25mm (1in) intervals using a waterproof marker.

4 Carefully dampen the back of the completed canvas using a hand spray which sprays with a soft mist (not a jet).

5 With the work right side up, stretch and pin one side into position, lining it up with the grid. Carefully pull it straight, keeping the corners square, and secure with the pins or staples placed close together, about 25mm (1in) away from the finished design. Repeat on the opposite side, then the other two sides.

6 You might have to readjust the canvas and reposition the pins as you work, so do not push them in completely until you are sure the work is square and straight.

7 Leave the board flat and allow the work to dry away from direct heat.

8 When the piece is completely dry, remove the pins and trim off the excess canvas to about ten threads. It is then ready to be mounted and framed or finished as described in the project.

Canvas Work Stitches

The traditional stitches given in this section are just a few of the many, wonderfully varied stitches found in canvas work embroidery. The projects are worked in wool, but stranded cotton (floss) or silk ribbon are included to 'lift' the design. The grid lines in the illustrations represent the canvas mesh and show clearly the order in which to work the stitch. I recommend counting the mesh and not the holes. Half or 'compensating' stitches are sometimes necessary to accommodate the shape of the design and the pattern of the stitch must remain correct. Keep an even tension to cover the canvas as you sew. Avoid distorting the canvas by pulling the thread too tightly.

Tent Stitch

Tent stitch (probably the most used canvas work stitch) is a single diagonal stitch worked in lines (Fig. 2-5). Whatever the direction, it is important to work with a long stitch on the back – this creates a rich hard-wearing stitch which gives good coverage. Tent stitch worked in single lines horizontally, diagonally or vertically is known as continental tent stitch. Working continental tent stitch can distort the canvas so, wherever possible, work diagonal tent stitch (basketweave).

Always start tent stitch with a waste knot, and finish off by bringing the wool to the surface. Try not to finish off by weaving your thread through the back of tent stitches as this can cause unsightly ridges and spoils the tension (if this is unavoidable, split up the strands and take them separately through the back in different directions).

1 Practise a few small samples of continental tent stitch following the order shown by the lettering and you will quickly understand the importance of the long stitch on the back.

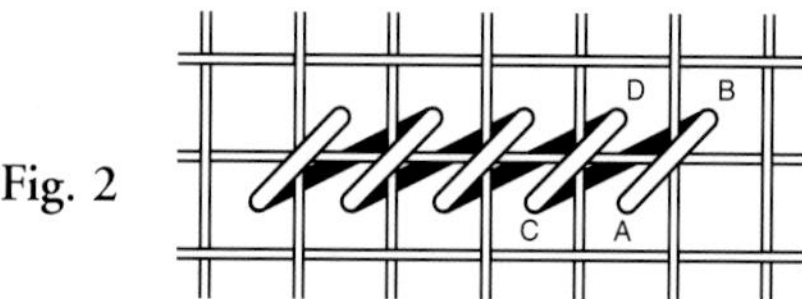

Tent stitch worked from right to left

2 When you turn a corner or change direction, avoid making a half cross stitch (without a long stitch on the back) on the return journey by mistake. The difference in technique will show on the front of the work.

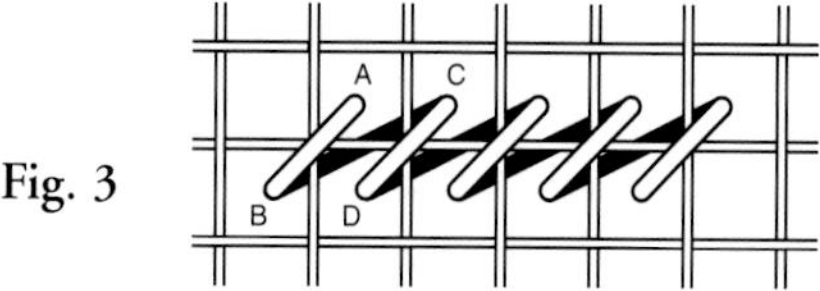

Tent stitch worked from left to right

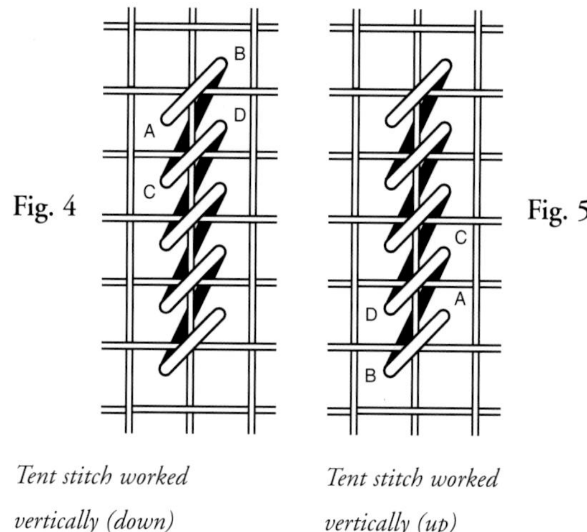

Tent stitch worked vertically (down)

Tent stitch worked vertically (up)

Diagonal Tent Stitch (Basketweave)

This stitch (Fig. 6-8) looks the same as continental tent stitch on the front, although it is not worked in single lines but diagonally across the canvas, up and down, forming a basketweave effect on the back. It does not distort the canvas and wears well.

The best results are achieved by working with the weave of the canvas. If you can master the following method your stitches will interlock neatly without ridges and you will be able to work anywhere on the canvas. It is well worth stitching a small practice piece to develop confidence in changing direction.

1 Study the canvas and you will see that the mesh has one row with a vertical canvas thread on top of a horizontal one, and the next row has a horizontal thread on top of a vertical one (Fig. 6). You will be stitching diagonally up and down the canvas depending on which thread of the mesh is lying on the top.

Fig. 6

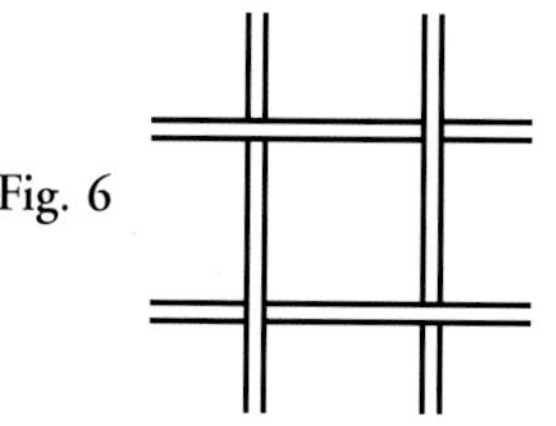

2 Ascend on a row which has a horizontal thread on top. Work the first diagonal stitch and take the needle behind two vertical canvas threads, ready to make a stitch over the next intersection up on the diagonal (Fig. 7).

Fig. 7

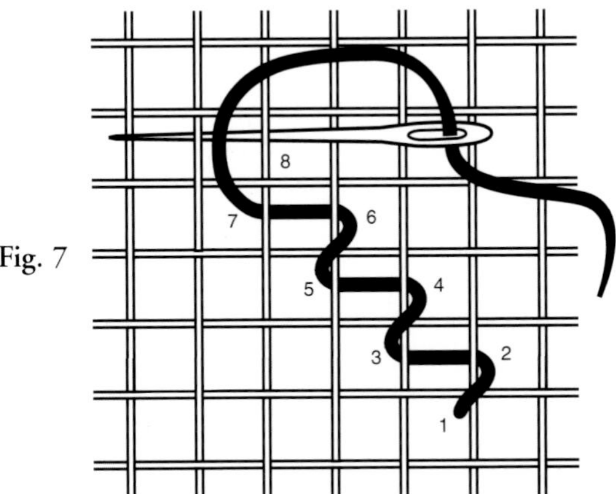

3 Descend on a row which has a vertical thread on top. Work the first diagonal stitch and take the needle behind two horizontal threads, ready to make a stitch over the next intersection down on the diagonal (Fig. 8).

Fig. 8

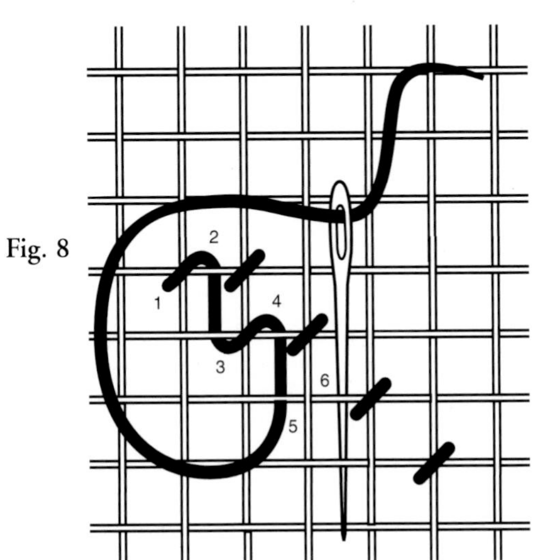

4 When working on a project, start in the top right-hand corner, check which canvas thread is on top after the first stitch, and continue ascending or descending accordingly.

Straight Gobelin Star

Keep an even tension when working the straight stitches of this solid motif (Fig. 9).

Fig. 9

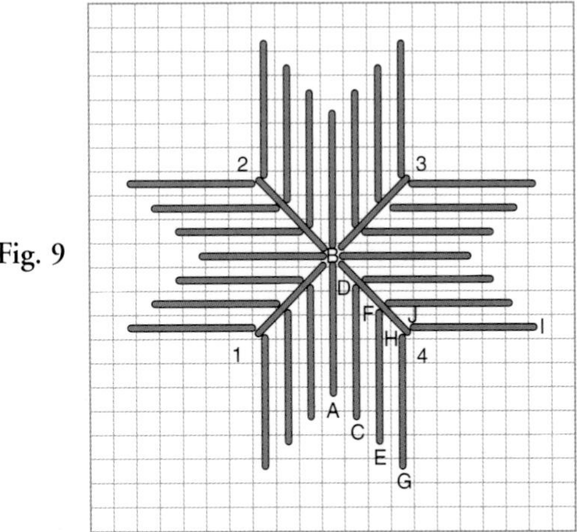

1 Start working this upright stitch at A over six threads, stepping each stitch by one thread as you proceed round the motif. It can be worked in a clockwise or anti-clockwise direction.

2 Complete with a diagonal stitch into the centre hole over all the right angles stitching 1B, 2B, 3B, 4B.

Half Gobelin Star

As above, ensure an even tension to achieve uniformity.

Fig. 10

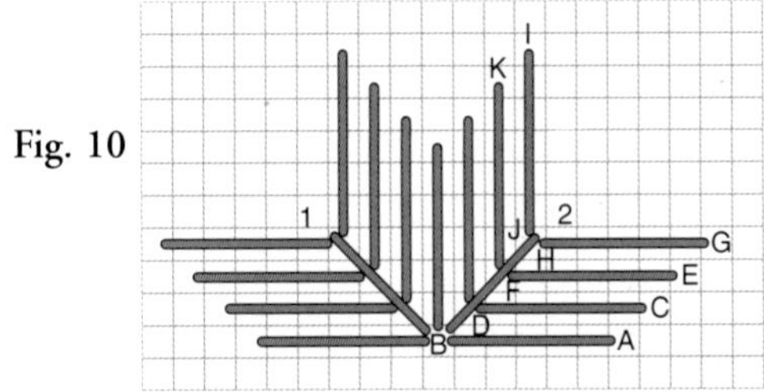

1 Work anti-clockwise round the motif from the side starting at A.

2 Complete with a diagonal stitch into the centre hole over all the right angles, stitching 1B, 2B.

Basic Cross Stitch

There are many different ways of working this quick stitch (Fig. 11), but most importantly the top stitches must always lie in the same direction. I suggest that you complete each stitch indivdually.

Fig. 11

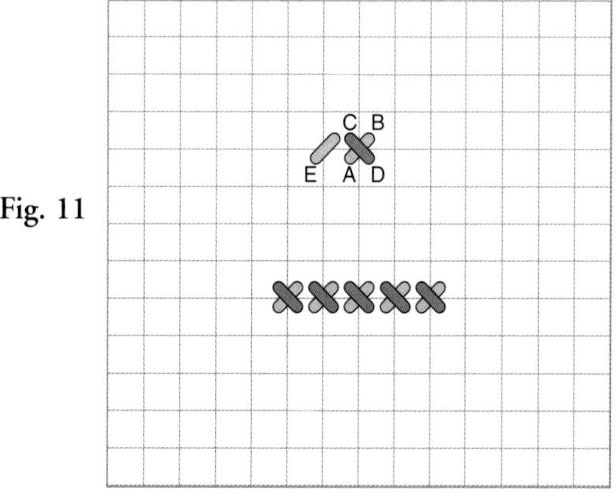

1 Bring the needle to the surface at A and down at B over one thread.

2 Come back to the surface at C and down at D and start again for the next stitch.

Upright Cross Stitch

This is an excellent textured stitch (Fig. 12) which can be worked singly, in rows, or diagonally.

Fig. 12

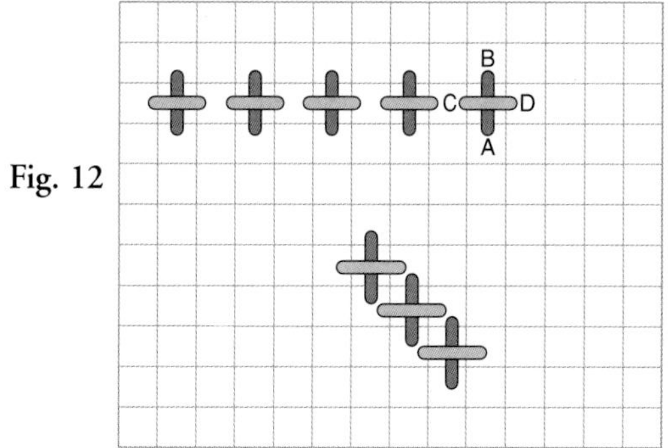

1 Work an upright straight stitch over 2 threads.

2 Cross this stitch with a horizontal one. It is important to be consistent as to which stitch lies on the surface.

3 It can be worked from left to right or right to left.

Rice Stitch (Crossed Corners Stitch)

Use this textured stitch (Fig. 13) for an outline or border, or to fill an area, working over two or four threads of canvas.

Fig. 13

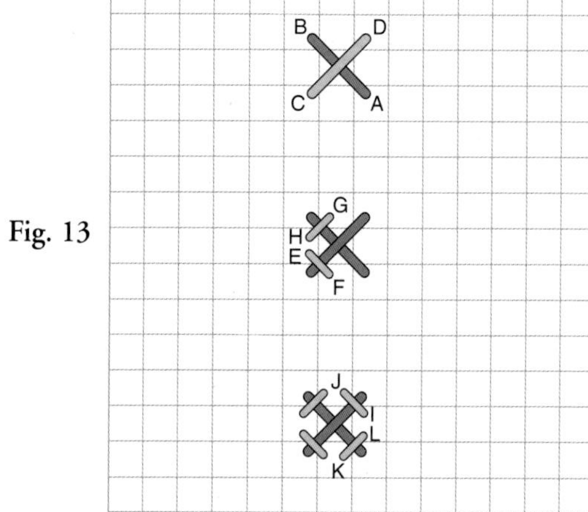

1 Begin with a diagonal cross stitch over two threads AB and CD.

2 Return up through the hole at E and take a small back stitch over the arm (CD) to F.

3 Bring the needle through at G, taking the back stitch over the arm (BA) to H.

4 Bring the needle through at I, taking the back stitch over the arm (DC) to J.

5 Bring the needle through at K and finish over the arm (AB) at L.

Hungarian Stitch

Used as a background, this attractive stitch (Fig. 14) will cover the canvas quickly and give an interesting texture.

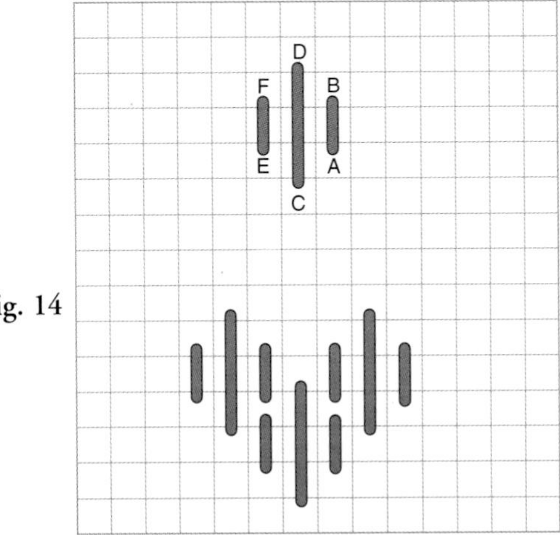

Fig. 14

1 Work groups of three straight stitches over two, four and two canvas threads with a space of two threads between.

2 Work in horizontal rows from left to right and right to left.

3 Slot the subsequent rows into the spaces between the preceding groups.

4 Neaten the top and bottom lines of an area using small compensating stitches.

Alicia's Lace

This reversing tent stitch (Fig. 15) is worked diagonally up and down the canvas, not in straight lines, to achieve a delicate lacy effect. It is especially attractive as a filling using space-dyed threads.

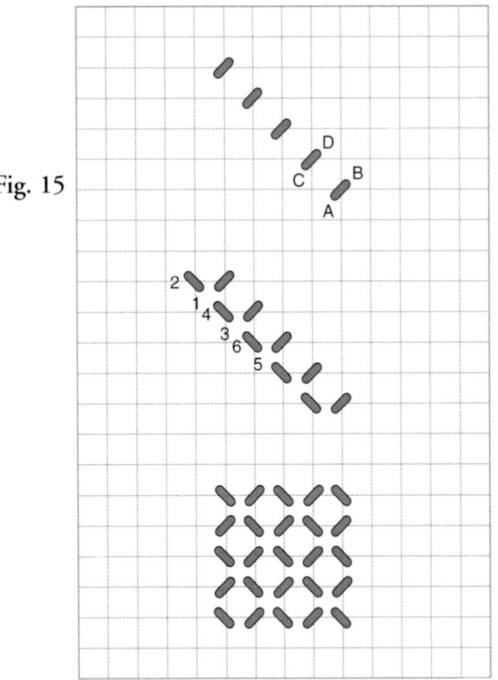

Fig. 15

1 First work a diagonal row of tent stitches up the canvas.

2 Back stitch diagonally down on the return journey over one thread.

3 Repeat lines one and two until the area is filled.

Straight Gobelin Stitch (Satin Stitch/Upright Gobelin Stitch)

One of the easiest stitches to do, this works well as a border or outline (Fig. 16). It can be worked vertically or horizontally over two, three, four or more canvas threads.

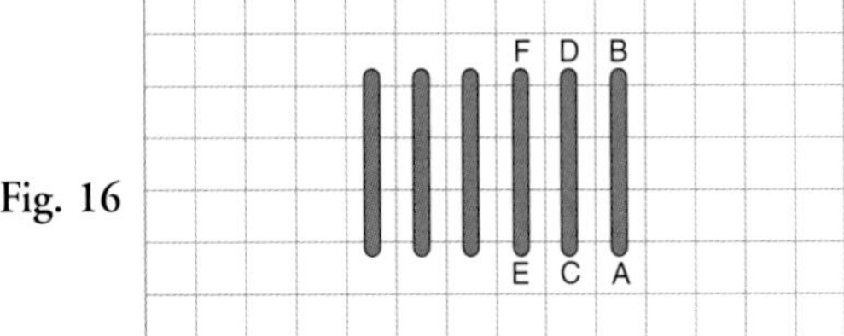

Fig. 16

1 Work from right to left or left to right.

2 Keep stitches even and with a fairly loose tension so that canvas threads do not show through.

3 If necessary, use a back stitch to cover any canvas showing at the edge.

Back Stitch

This is a useful stitch (Fig. 17) for definition or for covering canvas threads where they show through unintentionally. It is generally used over one or two threads.

Fig. 17

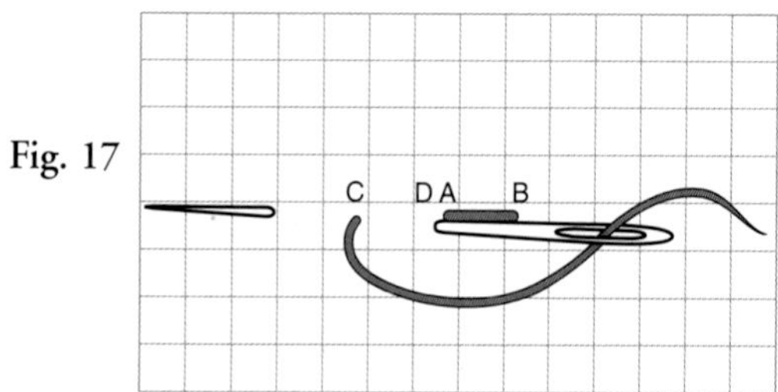

1 Bring the needle up at A and back over two threads to go down at B.

2 Come back up through the work at C, down at D and repeat the process.

Mosaic Stitch

This excellent neat background stitch (Fig. 18) forms a small box. It can be worked across the canvas, vertically or diagonally.

1 Work three diagonal stitches over one, two and one intersections to form a square over two threads of canvas.

Fig. 18

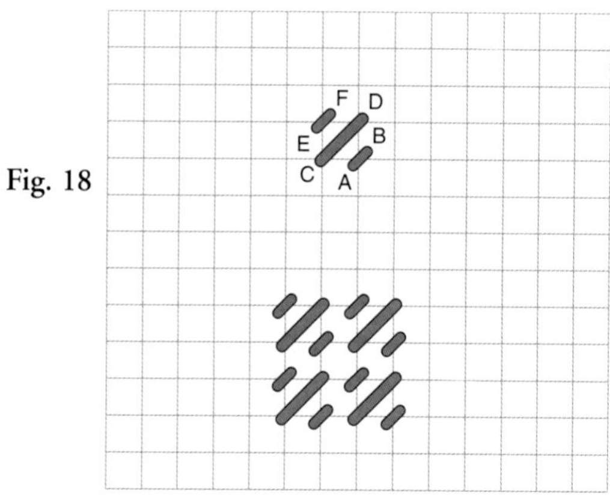

Reversed Mosaic

A variation of mosaic stitch (Fig. 19), this stitch creates an interesting texture. Where four squares meet there is space for including an upright cross stitch, small bead or French knot if appropriate. Work as for mosaic stitch, but reverse each square.

Fig. 19

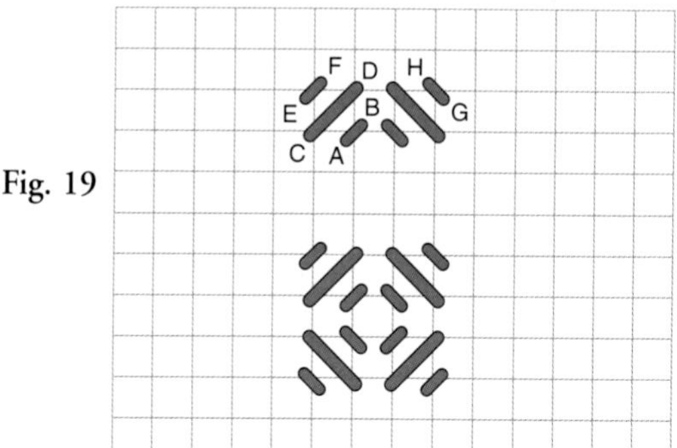

Diagonal Mosaic Stripe

Worked diagonally, this further variation of mosaic stitch (Fig. 20) is particularly useful for creating interesting effects when changing direction.

1 Work as for mosaic stitch, but keep going diagonally.

2 Separate each line of diagonal mosaic with a single tent stitch.

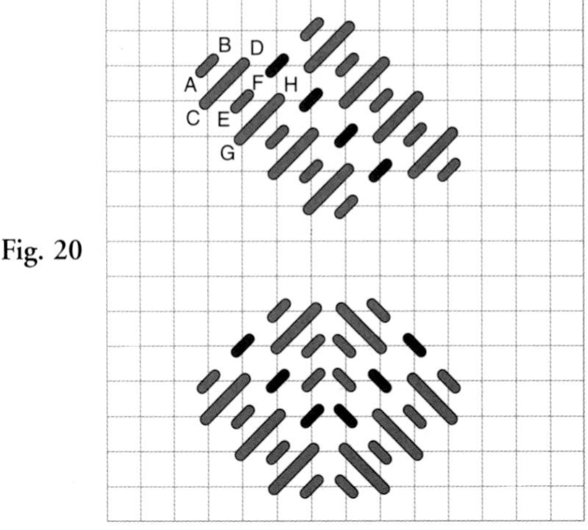

Fig. 20

3 Compensating tent stitches will be necessary when changing directions.

Double Stitch

This stitch (Fig. 21) has a bumpy appearance and works well as a border or a filling stitch, particularly when the small crosses are worked with silks, stranded cotton (floss), or space-dyed threads.

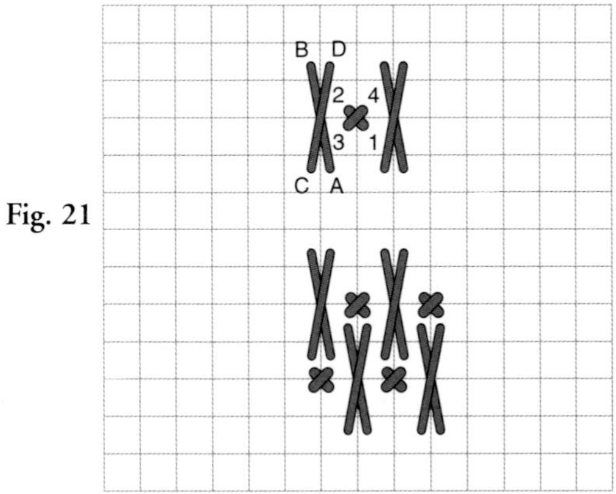

Fig. 21

1 Work a long cross stitch up over three threads and diagonally over one thread, leaving a single thread between each cross.

2 Overlap the next row as shown in Fig. 21.

3 Stitch the small crosses over one thread once the larger crosses have been established, keeping the top stitch facing the same way throughout.

4 Work a small compensating cross stitch at the top and bottom of the stitched area to neaten the edges.

Diagonal Satin Stitch

When worked in lines this stitch (Fig. 22) is smooth in appearance and works well as a border outline or to offset a textured stitch. Satin stitch can be worked vertically, horizontally, diagonally or reversed.

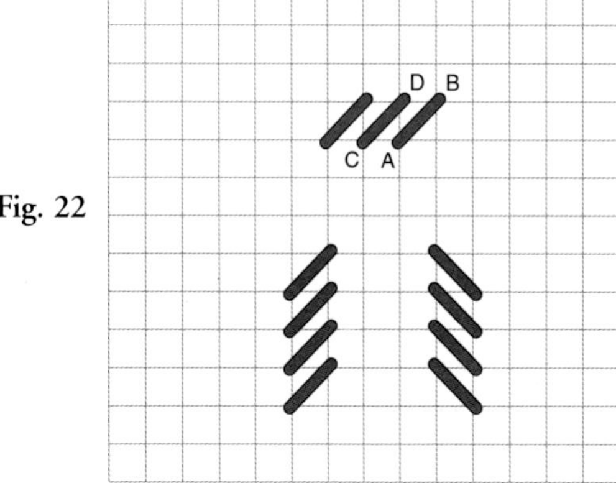

Fig. 22

1 Take a stitch diagonally over two threads and repeat.

2 Make a small compensating tent stitch at the beginning and end to cover the bare intersection.

Three-step Diagonal Satin Stitch with Mosaic (Diagonal Hungarian Ground)

This is an effective combination of stitches (Fig. 23), which gives scope for using lots of different colours and textures of threads.

Fig. 23

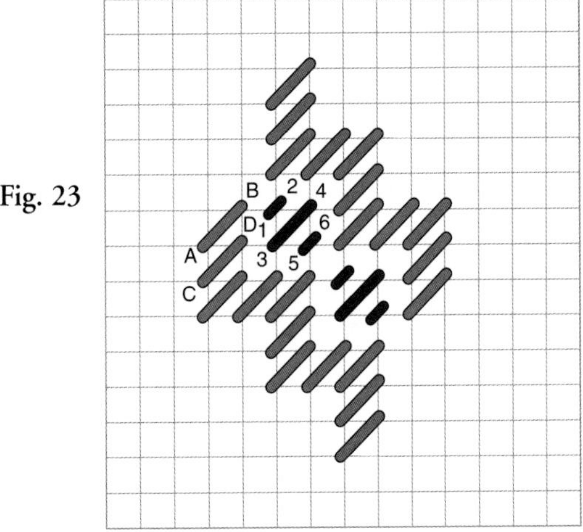

1 Work the diagonal satin stitches in zigzag steps.

2 Alternate mosaic stitch with the satin stitches to fill in the spaces.

Double Straight Cross

This is an excellent textured stitch (Fig. 24) which can be worked straight or diagonally.

Fig. 24

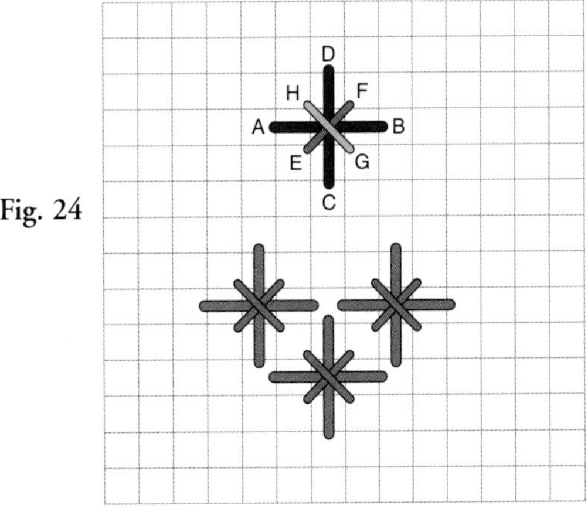

1 Work an upright cross stitch over four threads.

2 Work the small diagonal cross at the intersection over two threads. Make sure the top stitch is always facing the same way.

3 Slot subsequent rows into the spaces between the preceding groups.

Long-armed Cross Stitch (Long-legged Cross Stitch)

With the appearance of a twisted rope, this stitch (Fig. 25) works very successfully as a border, outline or filling stitch.

Fig. 25

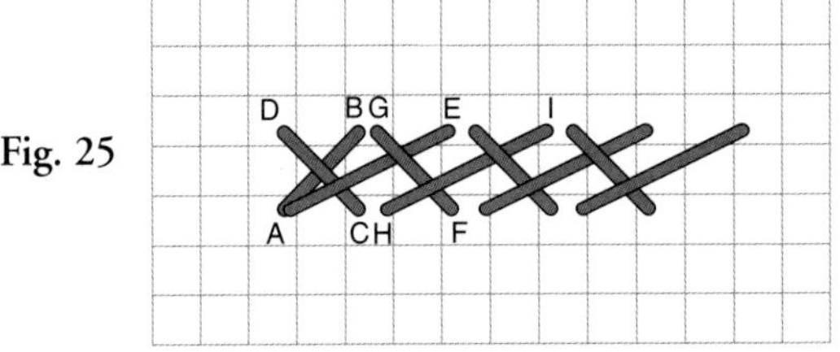

1 Start and finish with a basic cross stitch over two threads (to cover the canvas).

2 Come back through at A with a long stitch taken diagonally to E (across four threads and up two), come up at F and back diagonally over the arm (two threads) to G.

3 Come up at H and repeat the process.

Smyrna Cross

Consisting of a diagonal cross covered with an upright cross, this raised and textured stitch (Fig. 26) is particularly useful for an outline or border. It can be worked over two or four threads of canvas.

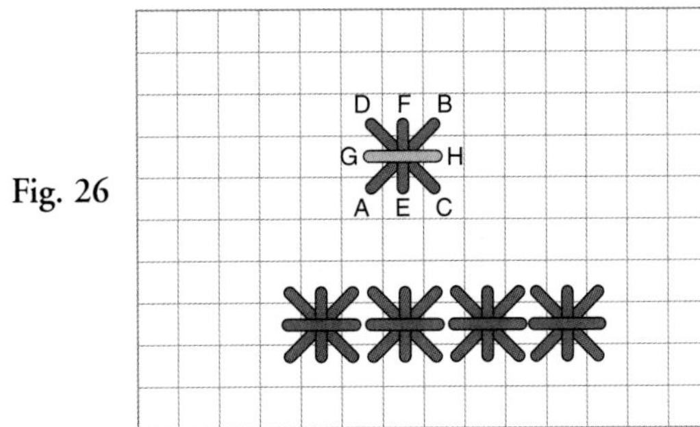

Fig. 26

1 Work the diagonal cross over two threads, AB, CD.

2 Cover with an upright cross stitch, making sure all the top stitches are worked in the same direction.

Cushion Stitch

Forming a small square when worked, this is one of the most basic and useful of all canvas stitches (Fig. 27), with numerous variations. The square formed by the stitch can be reversed or worked across the canvas vertically or diagonally.

Work five diagonal stitches over one, two, three, two and one intersections to form a square over four threads of canvas.

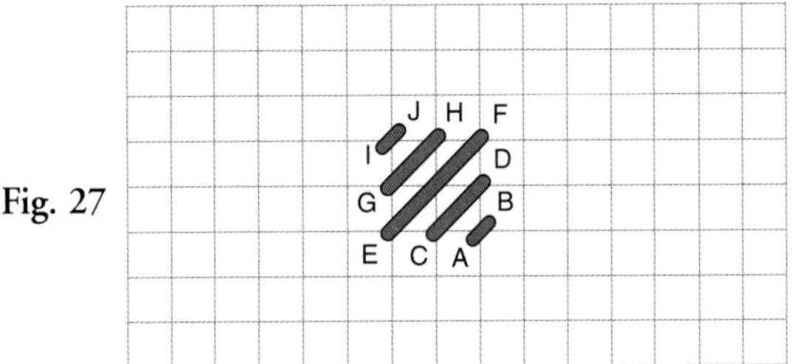

Fig. 27

Ringed Eyelet Daisies with Double Straight Cross

These 'circular' eyelets look like flowers. They are separated by double straight cross and outlined with back stitch (Fig. 28).

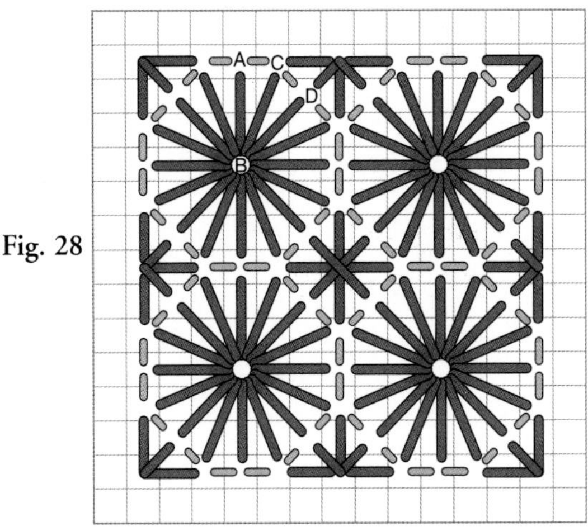

Fig. 28

1 Always work from the outside edge down into the centre of the stitch.

2 Work clockwise round the eyelet, starting from A.

3 Complete all the eyelets before filling in with the double straight cross.

4 Finish with the back stitch outline.

Heirloom Sewing

Fine fabrics, beautiful laces and basic machine stitching skills are the hallmarks of successful heirloom sewing. Delicate effects are easily achieved by joining laces and fabrics and the results are enormously rewarding. Although they are used mostly for garments, heirloom sewing skills can also enhance decorative items made for the home, where they are sure to be admired and appreciated.

The minimum requirement is a swing-needle sewing machine so that you can zigzag as well as straight stitch. The more exotic machine with built-in patterns is an agreeable bonus.

Fabric and Thread

Use the best-quality fabric that you can afford, whether it is fine lawns, wool, silk or cotton mixes and select the fabric most appropriate to the type of project you are undertaking. I have used pure cotton lawn for the projects in this book, for practicability and easy washing, but other materials could easily be substituted.

Use a fine cotton thread for machine stitching (eg, Mettler Cotton 60/2) to ensure that joined edges lie as flat as possible and to prevent extra bulk.

Lace

A wide selection of fine cotton laces are readily available and vary according to their uses. I have used the following types in the heirloom sewing projects.

Entredeux ('between two'): a Swiss embroidery lace resembling hem stitching and used to link laces and fabric.

Insertions: a fine cotton lace, flat edged on both sides, with straight thread headings.

Swiss beading lace: an insertion lace with slots for threading ribbon and a border of entredeux on either side of the design.

Edgings: one straight side with a heading and one scalloped edge, for use on hems, neck and sleeve.

Heirloom Sewing Techniques

Preparation

Always cut fabric along the straight grain. To determine the straight grain of the fabric, pull a thread along the edge. To make insertion laces easier to handle, spray starch them lightly and press.

French Seams

1 Place the fabric wrong sides together (ws) and stitch 6mm (¼in) from the edge (Fig. 1). Trim to 3mm (⅛in) and press the edges to one side.

Fig. 1

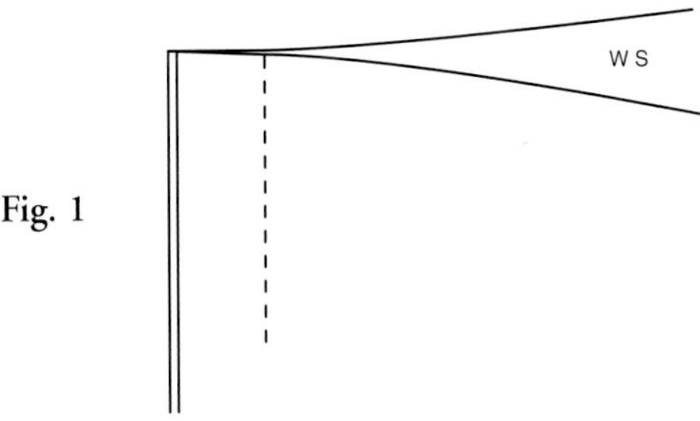

2 Open out the seam and bring right sides of fabric together (rs). Machine stitch along the seam again, 6mm (¼in) from the edge, thus encasing the original edges within the French seam (Fig 2).

Fig. 2

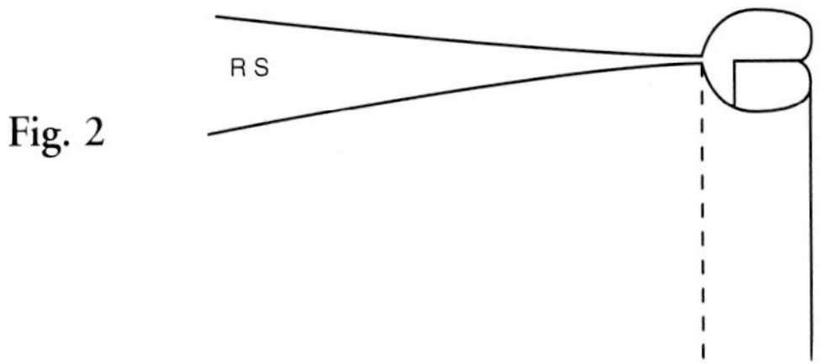

Setting Zigzag Lengths/Widths

To find the right length and width of zigzag, work a sample on a small piece of entredeux.

Fig. 3

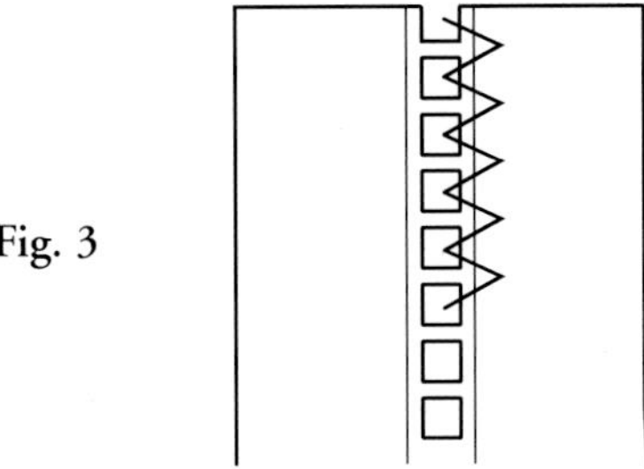

1 Adjust the width of the stitch until the left swing of the needle goes into the centre of the entredeux and the right swing hits the fabric of the entredeux. Alter the length of the stitch until the needle goes into a new hole with every swing. Make a note of these settings for the rest of your project (Fig. 3).

Joining Entredeux to Straight-edged Fabric

1 With the fabric and entredeux placed right sides together, join them by straightstitching near the holes. Trim the two fabric edges to 3mm (⅛in) (Fig. 4).

Fig. 4

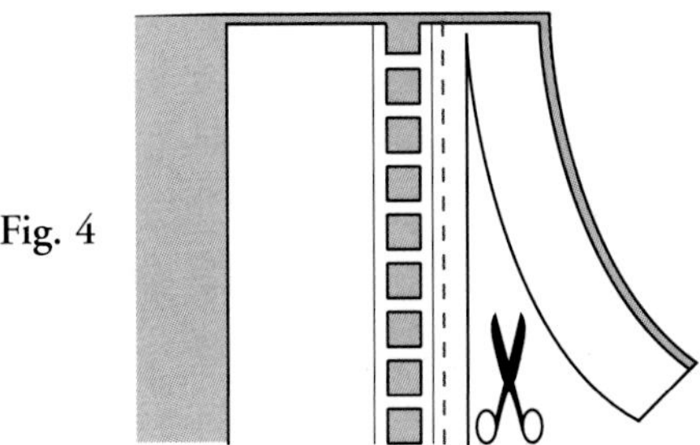

2 Return to your zigzag settings and machine off the edge and back over the straight stitching so that the two trimmed edges roll and whip together (Fig. 5).

Fig. 5

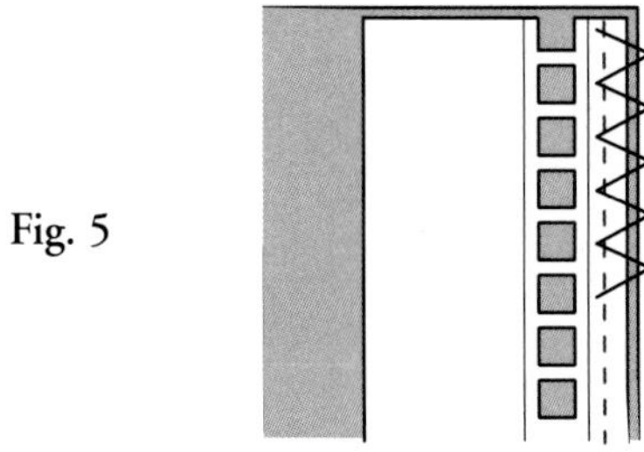

Joining Gathered Lace to Entredeux

1 Gather the lace by pulling the top thread in the heading, ensuring that the gathers are evenly spaced (Fig. 6).

Fig. 6

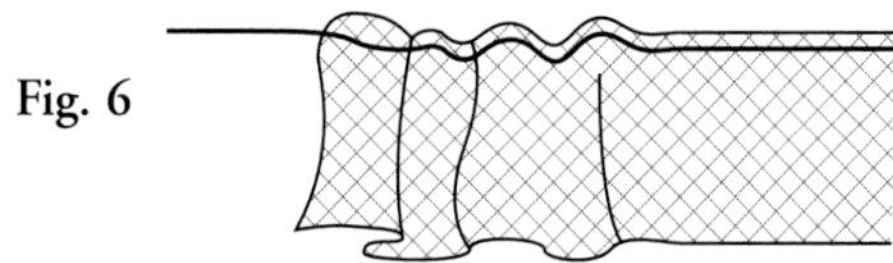

2 Trim one side of the entredeux (Fig. 7).

Fig. 7

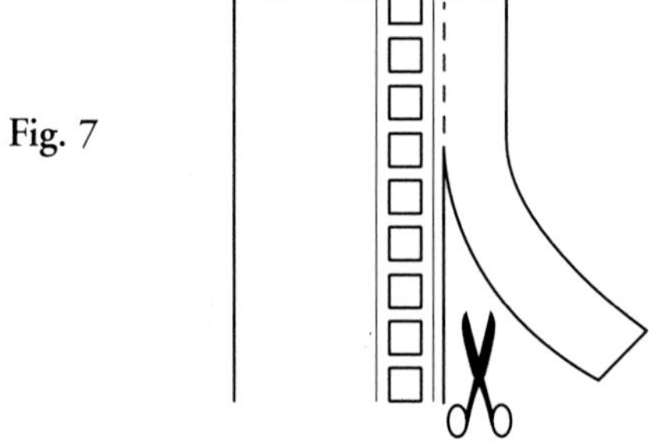

3 With right sides up, butt the gathered lace edge against the entredeux edge. Zigzag together, stitching off the edge and into each hole of the entredeux (Fig. 8), and incorporating the gathers and lace heading. It may be necessary to arrange the gathers into position as you stitch. Use a suitable implement and not your fingers!

Fig. 8

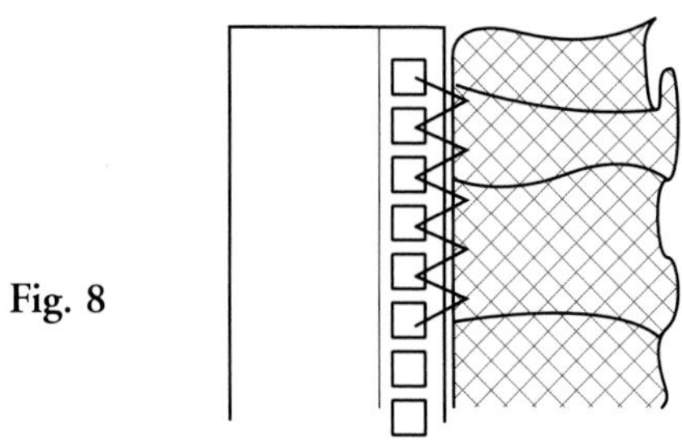

Joining Gathered Fabric to Entredeux

1 Machine stitch three rows of gathering lines on the edge of the fabric. Pull up the thread and adjust the gathers. With right sides of fabric and entredeux together, straightstitch close to the holes (Fig.9).

Fig. 9

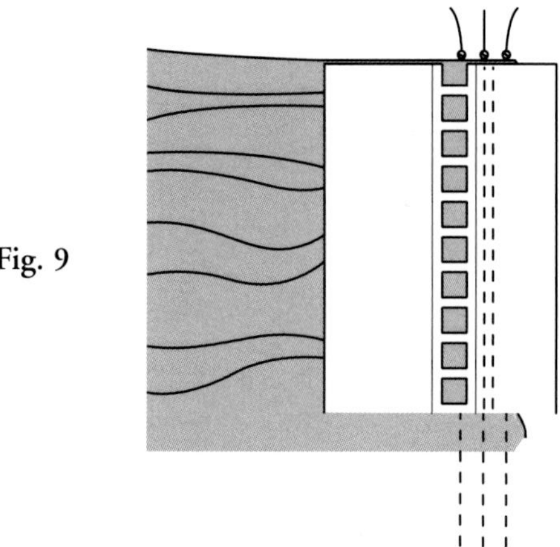

2 Shift the needle one position to the right and stitch another line. Trim the two fabric edges to 3mm (⅛in). Zigzag together, stitching off the edge and back over the straight stitching to roll and whip the edges together (Fig. 10).

Fig. 10

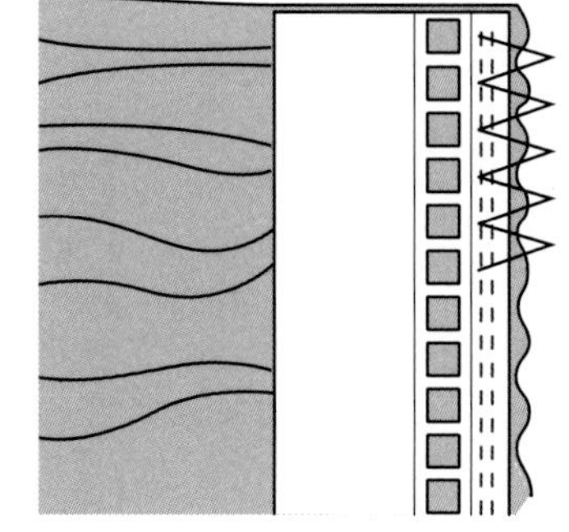

Joining Lace to Flat Fabric

1 Lightly starch and press the lace, trimming any loose threads. With right sides together, position the lace on the fabric, 3-6mm (⅛-¼in) from the edge of the fabric (Fig. 11).

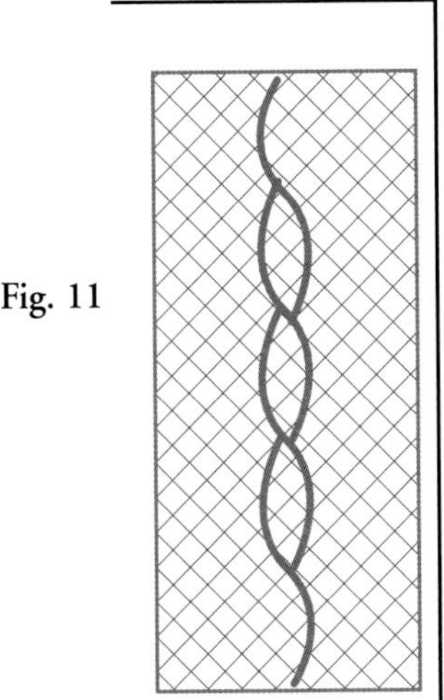

Fig. 11

2 Zigzag stitch the lace and fabric together, stitching off the fabric edge so that the edges roll and whip together (Fig. 12).

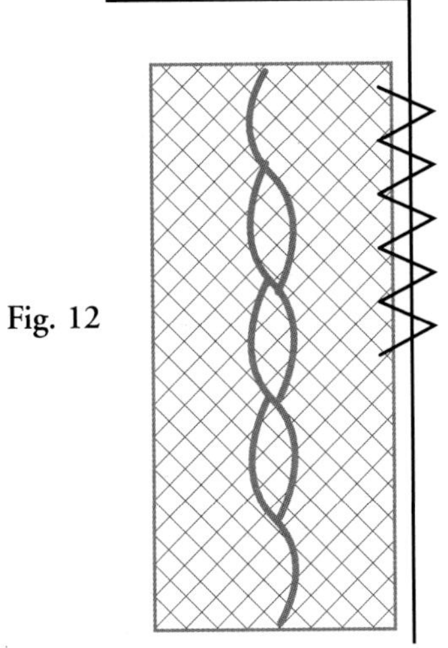

Fig. 12

Joining Entredeux to Straight-edged Lace

1 Lightly starch and press the lace. Trim one side of the entredeux and butt this edge against the lace edge, right sides up (Fig. 13).

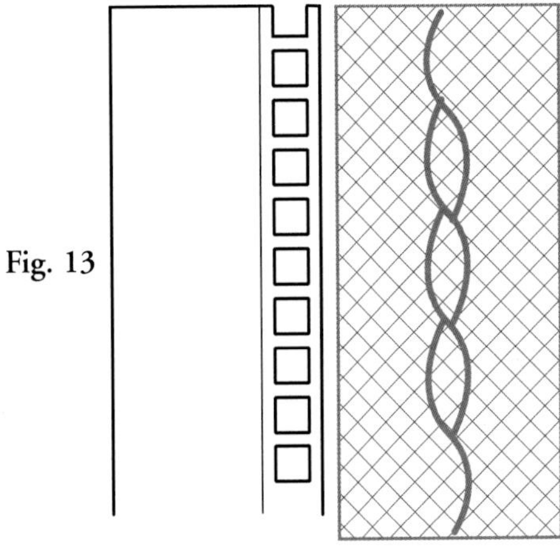

Fig. 13

2 Zigzag stitch the two together, adjusting the length of the stitch so that the needle goes into the entredeux holes and is wide enough to enclose the lace heading (Fig. 14).

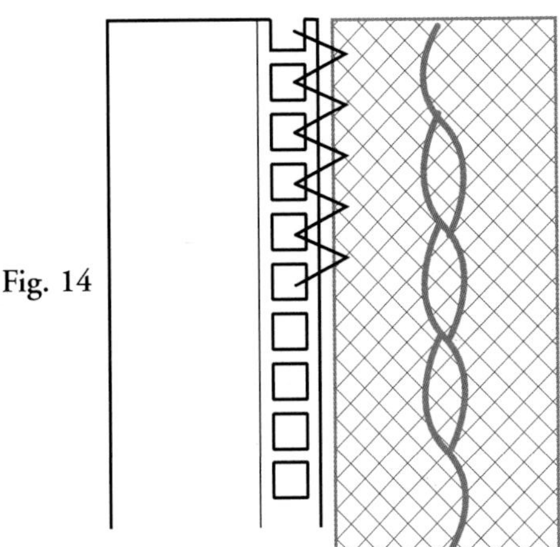

Fig. 14

HARDANGER EMBROIDERY

The distinctive Norwegian embroidery technique of Hardanger is a form of cut and drawn work, which has roots in Italian Reticella lace. Norway has a rich tradition of regional folk dress and this beautiful embroidery is characteristically worked in white thread on crisp white cotton or linen for the aprons, shirts and kerchiefs of the Hardanger 'bunad' (folk dress).

The main features of Hardanger embroidery are the satin-stitch blocks (Kloster blocks) which form the design, and needleweaving (Stoppesaum) worked over the grid left behind after the cutting and withdrawal of threads. More ornate filling stitches enhance the lacy effects, with traditional solid satin-stitch motifs giving depth and substance to the geometric designs.

Fabric

Hardanger embroidery is worked on an evenweave fabric. You will be spending valuable time creating an heirloom for future generations, so always buy a good-quality fabric. I prefer to use linen, although there is an evenweave cotton called Hardanger fabric and other cotton-mix evenweaves available. There is also a wide range of colours to be found.

Fabrics for the Hardanger projects can easily be painted to match a particular colour scheme. In addition to the usual fabric paints, there is a non-toxic spray paint called Delta Colour Accents which has a wide colour range and is easy to use.

Threads

Two sizes of DMC Coton Perlé are used for the Hardanger projects in this book. Kloster blocks and surface motifs and border stitches are worked in Coton Perlé No. 8. Needleweaving, pulled-thread stitches (eyelets, reversed diagonal faggoting, hem stitching) and infilling stitches are worked with Coton Perlé No. 12.

Linen thread could also be used. To decide the correct thickness of linen thread, withdraw a thread from your fabric and lay it beside your stitching threads. For the heavier work, choose a thread which is slightly thicker than the thread from the fabric, and for the finer work choose a thread which is slightly thinner. Do not forget to make quantity adjustments if you choose to work with linen thread.

All the Hardanger projects in this book could be worked with space-dyed thread. Never be afraid to experiment, as there is a wonderfully exciting assortment of space-dyed threads in varying thicknesses. Choose the correct thickness as for linen thread, but also check for colour fastness. When joining lengths of space-dyed thread, remember to cut from the same end of the skein, so that the colours follow on. I suggest working a small practise piece to check the effect.

Equipment

Good-quality embroidery scissors with fine, sharp points are essential to cut the threads neatly. Use blunt-ended tapestry needles size 24 with both sizes of Coton Perlé. The use of an embroidery hoop is not recommended as it restricts movement.

Preparing to Work

1 Neaten the edges of the linen by pulling a thread and cutting straight along this line.

2 Oversew or machine zigzag the edges of the linen to prevent it fraying.

3 Find the centre of the fabric by folding in half and gently creasing, first in one direction and then the other.

4 Mark the centre fold lines with a line of tacking (basting) stitches in a pastel-coloured thread.

Starting and Finishing

Secure the thread with an away-knot (see page 10) on the surface of linen, 8cm (3in) from the side of your initial stitch. Once the stitches are completed, cut off the knot, re-thread the tail of cotton and weave through the back of completed stitches, taking two or three small back stitches to secure.

As a general rule, to fasten off go to the back and slip through completed stitches, fixing with a few small back stitches. To finish off Kloster blocks, take the thread to the back and slip through the 'tunnels' formed by the blocks. Come up through a block and take a back stitch over the middle thread. Hold tightly and pull to set the stitch firmly in position. Repeat in the subsequent two blocks to ensure the thread is secure before cutting off.

Keeping your Work Clean

To keep the work clean, store it in a protective bag or pillow case. If necessary, wash the finished embroidery by hand using a mild soap powder. Dry it face down on towelling, stretching it carefully into shape. Press from the back onto a soft cloth while damp.

Hardanger Stitches

Kloster Blocks (Klostersaum)

Worked at right angles to each other or in straight lines, Kloster blocks (Fig. 1) consist of five straight stitches worked over four threads of the fabric. They outline the design and are always worked with the thicker thread.

Fig. 1

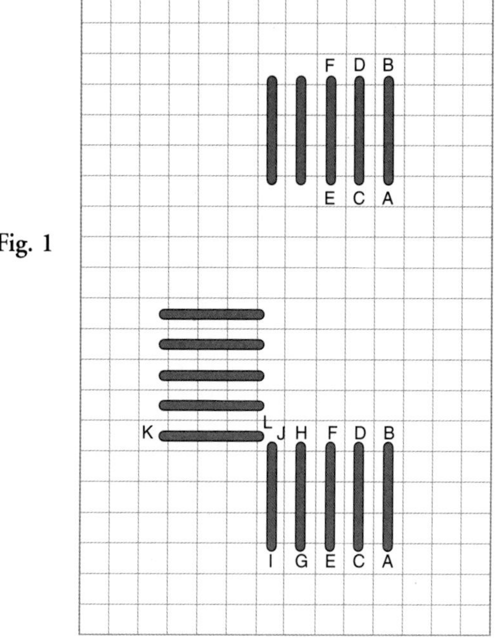

1 Start with an away-waste knot on the surface.

2 Come up through the fabric at A and take a stitch over four threads as shown. Always start and finish at one end of a block and not in the middle.

3 Pull the stitch to sit comfortably on the surface of the fabric, but not so tightly as to bunch and distort the linen threads.

4 As you stitch designs, keep checking that the Kloster blocks are lined up correctly (in all directions) and that you have not miscounted somewhere.

5 Once you have established some blocks, you will be able to start threads as you finish them (see page 25).

6 Always outline the design completely with Kloster blocks before going on to any other part of the design.

Square Eyelet (Dronningsting)

As well as being decorative, when used with buttonhole edging, eyelets help to strengthen the edges (Fig. 2). Use fine thread and work over two threads of the fabric.

Fig. 2

1 Work clockwise, bringing the needle up from the outside corner at A and down through the centre hole B.

2 Hold the eyelet and pull the thread gently away from the centre towards the edge to form a hole. Repeat until the eyelet is complete.

3 To finish, take the thread to the wrong side, (pulling away from the centre hole) and go through the back of the blocks, taking a

backstitch as with the Kloster blocks.

4 For eyelets with buttonhole edging, complete the first eyelet and move to subsequent eyelets by slipping the threads through the blocks (on the wrong side). Start each successive eyelet at the same point, but one square further on.

5 For a half eyelet, stitch as before, but stop at the half way point (Fig. 2, bottom).

6 To ensure the fine thread is securely started and finished off, weave carefully through the back of already completed stitches, anchor the thread with a back stitch and pull tightly to prevent it slipping.

Diagonal Eyelets

Diagonal eyelets (Fig. 3) are delicate and decorative, giving an open, lacy look, especially good next to a heavier motif. And it is not as difficult as it looks. Work over two threads and pull gently away from the middle to the sides as you proceed round.

1 Stitch clockwise round the outside of all four small eyelets (Fig. 3, top), starting at A and stitching down into the centre hole B.

2 Proceed C > B, D > B, E > B, F > B, back to F, F > G. Continue to K > G, back to K, K > L and continue to P > L, back to P, P > Q, R > Q, S > Q, T > Q, A > Q.

3 When you reach Q continue round the inside of the eyelet, (Fig. 3, middle) anticlockwise, U > Q, V > Q, W > Q back to W. Stitch W > L and continue until complete (Fig. 3, bottom).

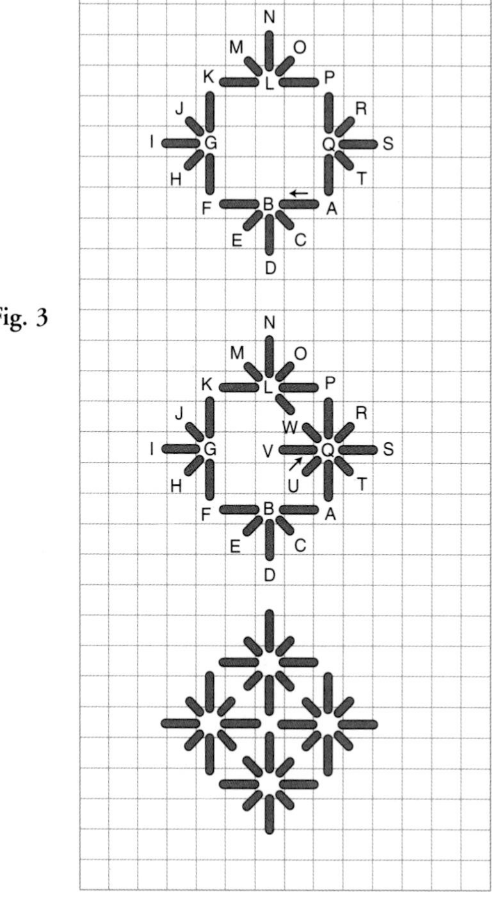

Fig. 3

Reversed Diagonal Faggoting Stitch (Vestmannarenning)

This pulled-thread stitch (Fig. 4) with its open effect works beautifully as an outline definition to the Kloster blocks. Practise this stitch on some spare fabric before using it.

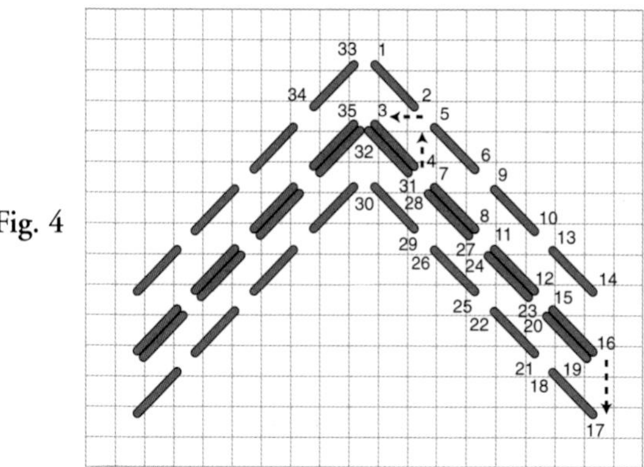

Fig. 4

1 Secure the thread and bring the needle up through the fabric, commencing at 1.

2 Work diagonally over two threads as shown for the required number of stitches.

3 For the return journey, turn the work upside down and repeat, going over the centre line a second time.

4 Pull gently after each stitch to create the open effect, holding the stitch so the work does not twist and making sure that the threads lie side by side and not on top of each other.

5 Check that the stitches line up opposite each other in all directions.

Satin Stitch Stars

Stars (Figs. 5-6) are characteristic of Hardanger embroidery, adding texture and depth against the lacy effects of other stitches. Always stitch each star separately and do not carry threads from one motif to another.

1 Commence at 1.

2 Complete one point as shown in Fig. 5, take thread through to the back and come up to the front at 23.

Fig. 5

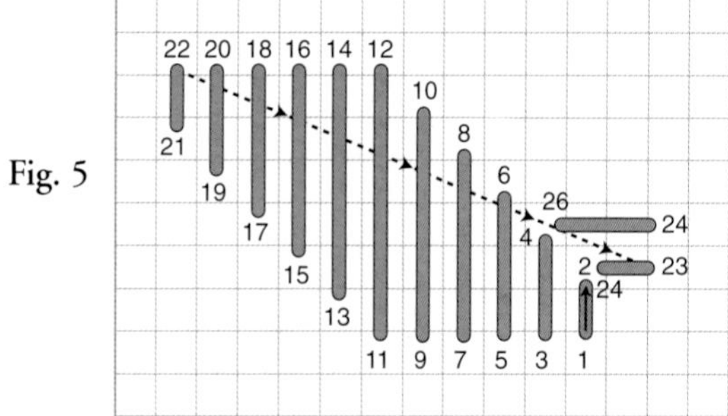

3 Continue to form either a half or whole star (Fig. 6).

Fig. 6

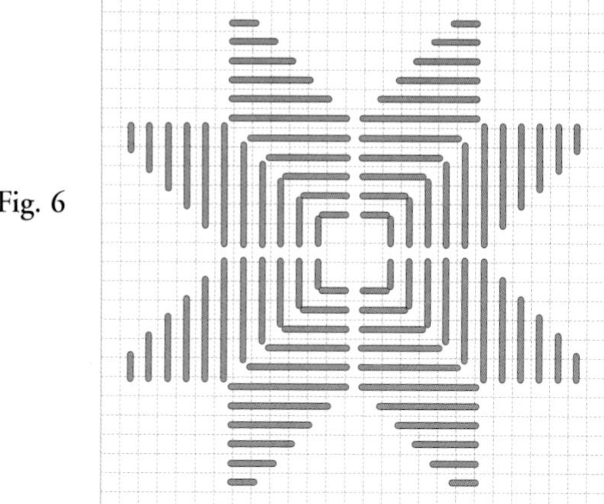

4 Where possible, when stitches share the same hole, stab down into the hole to keep threads lying smoothly and try not to pull your satin stitches too tightly.

5 If appropriate, work a small eyelet in the centre of the star.

Cutting

Don't be afraid to cut! After the threads have been cut (Fig. 7) you will be left with a grid of four threads to needleweave. Complete the Kloster blocks and all other surface embroidery before you cut the design.

Fig. 7

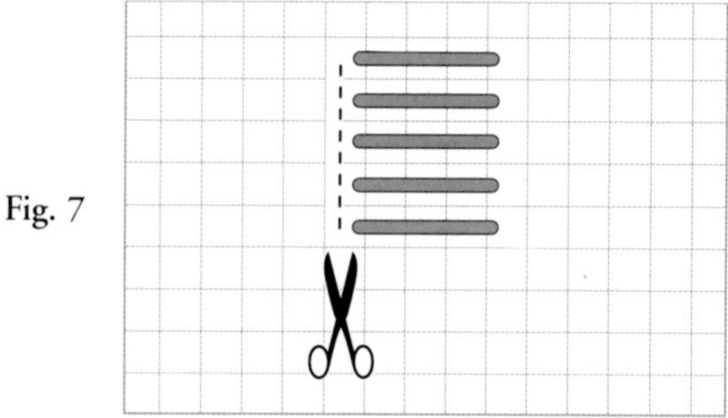

1 Cut four threads against the sides of the satin stitches and never at the 'open' end of the block.

2 When cutting the threads, position the scissors to the left of the satin stitches forming the Kloster block (Fig. 7).

3 Adjust the threads to be cut on the blades of the scissors and check you have the right number before cutting all four together. Never cut one at a time as you can easily snip an extra thread by mistake!

4 Cut one side of the design, turn the work and repeat the process on the opposite side.

5 Pull out the cut threads carefully.

6 Do not panic if you have cut a wrong thread by mistake. Merely pull out a thread of the linen from the side of your work and, following the weave of the cut thread, darn and re-weave your new thread into position beside the one you have snipped. Needleweave these two threads as one until secured.

Needleweaving the bars

It is important for the needlewoven bars to be uniform and straight.

Fig. 8

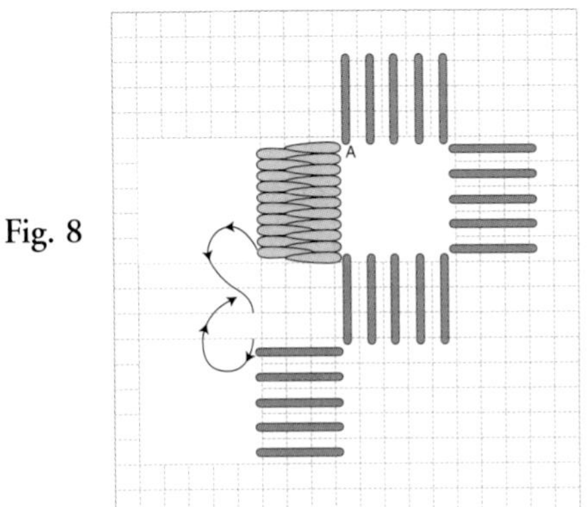

1 Come through to the front at A.

2 Work the bars by taking the needle down into the middle of the bar, weaving under and over two threads at a time in a figure of eight (Fig. 8). Hold the threads under your thumb as you stitch and pull tightly to achieve bars which have a neat and even tension.

3 Aim to complete the same number of stitches on each bar so the grid does not become distorted. Do not cram too many stitches on each bar as this will also distort the shape. Ensure you have enough thread to reach and finish off in a Kloster block.

4 On completing a bar, move to the next one, taking the needle behind from the far side of the completed bar, down into the centre of the next bar.

5 Work consistently across the design, in steps and not from bar to bar in the same row.

Dove's Eye Filling

The dove's eye (Figs. 9-10) can be worked either clockwise or anticlockwise, but it is important that all four sides should cross in the same way. Complete the needleweaving on three-and-a-half sides of a square of withdrawn threads before starting the dove's eye filling.

Fig. 9

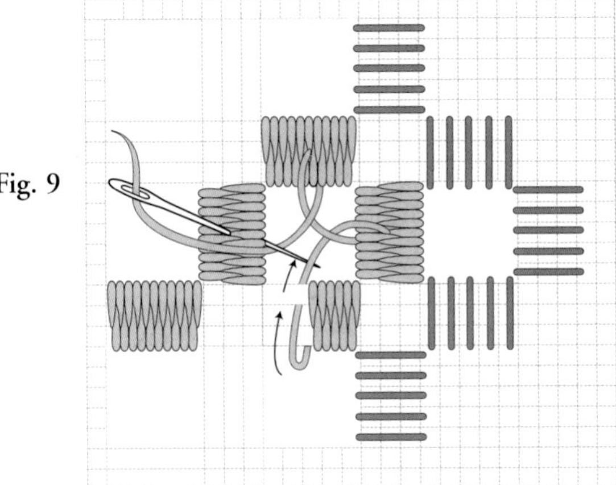

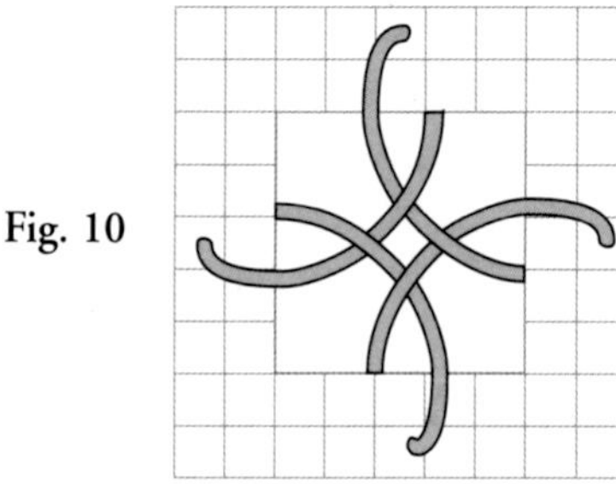

Fig. 10

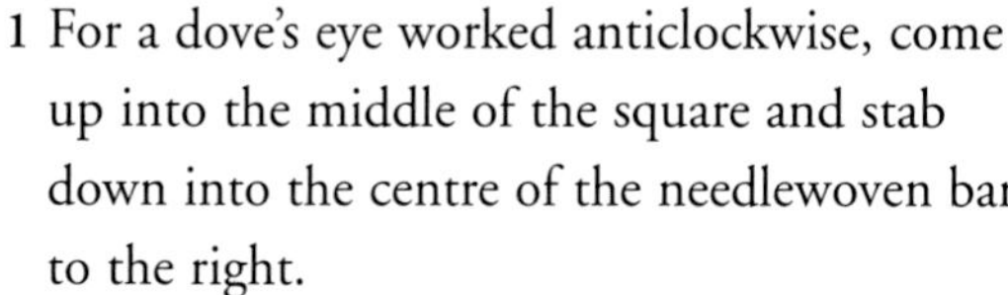

1 For a dove's eye worked anticlockwise, come up into the middle of the square and stab down into the centre of the needlewoven bar to the right.

2 Bring the thread up from underneath, loop over first thread, and down into the centre of the next bar to the right.

3 Adjust the shape of the loop and repeat the process to the fourth bar.

4 To finish, slip the thread under the first loop and back down into the middle to continue needleweaving the last half of the fourth bar, readjusting the shape if necessary. Aim to make the dove's eyes all the same size.

5 Reverse the process for working dove's eyes in a clockwise direction.

Woven Bars with Single French Knots

Single French knots (Figs. 11-12) worked in the middle of a woven bar on one or both sides add to the delicacy of a decorative filling. They may be also be used with other fillings.

1 Needleweave to the centre of the bar.

2 Wrap the thread once anticlockwise round the needle, before placing the needle down in the middle of the bar to work the next stitch. Hold the knot tightly in position while pulling the needle and thread through the centre to finish needleweaving the bar. Try not to jerk the thread as this can move the knot out of place.

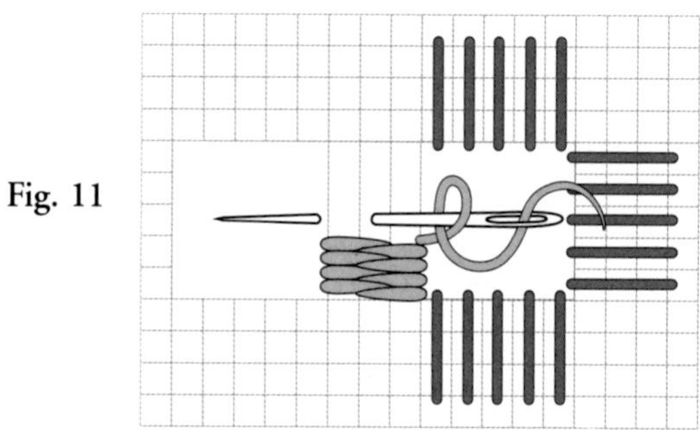

Fig. 11

3 For a knot on both sides of the bar, complete the first knot, stitch down into the centre of the bar to the other side and make the second knot (Fig. 12). Continue needleweaving the rest of the bar as before.

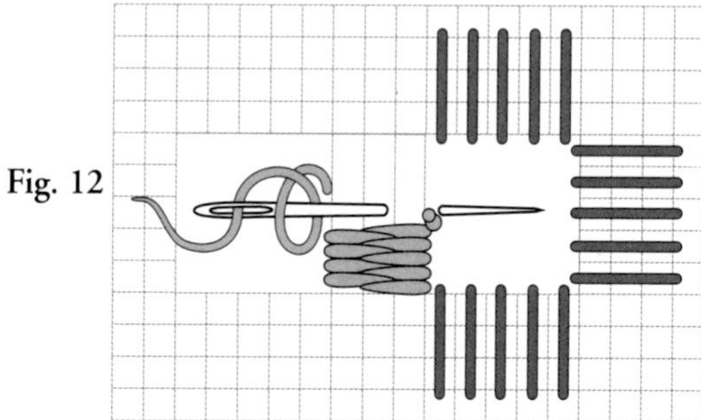

Fig. 12

Buttonhole Stitch Edging

This loop stitch (Figs. 13-16) is used to outline and enclose the edge of a design so that embroidery may be cut away from the background. Practical and decorative, it can also be used to give density and depth to an inner part of the design. If there is an inner row of Kloster blocks, work these before the buttonhole edging. Work from left to right.

Fig. 13

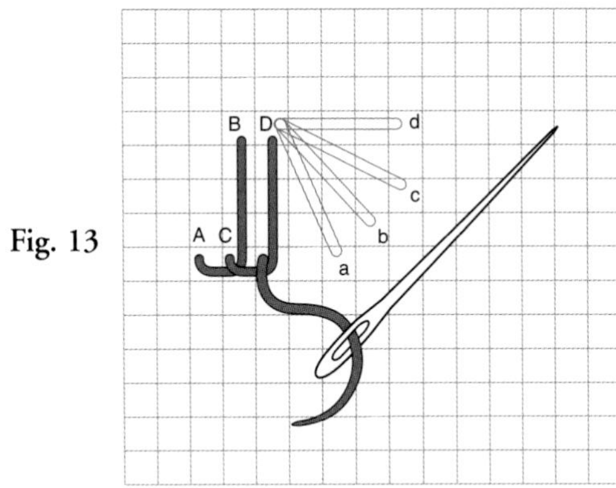

1 Secure the thread with a waste knot. Come up through the fabric at A, taking the needle down at B, one thread to the right of A and four threads up.

2 Before pulling tightly, come up at C within the loop AB. Pull up to lie neatly on the surface.

3 To turn a corner follow Fig. 13, leaving a space before coming up at a. Work three buttonhole stitches on the diagonal at a, b and c, going down into the corner hole (marked with a dot) each time. Leave another space before coming up at d to start the next block of buttonhole stitches. Five threads will be packed into the corner hole so do not pull too tightly as this will enlarge the area.

4 Always double check that you have correctly positioned the stitches at a, b, c and d. If it is difficult to find the right holes, gently push the previous stitch to one side to get your bearings.

5 For a right-angled corner bring the needle up through the fabric at E before forming a loop and continuing with the stitch (Figs. 14-15).

Fig. 14

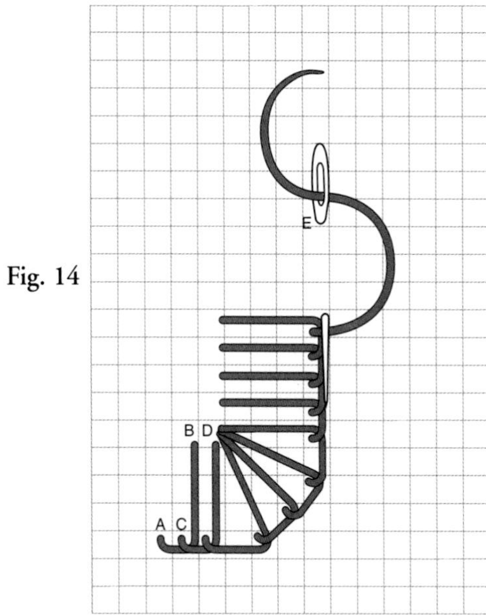

6 To start a new thread follow Fig. 15. It is important not to see any joins, so make the link in the middle of a block. Leave the old short thread to one side and join in a new one, weaving through the back, taking one or two back stitches to secure. Bring the needle through at Y and make a buttonhole loop in the next space. Continue stitching.

Fig. 15

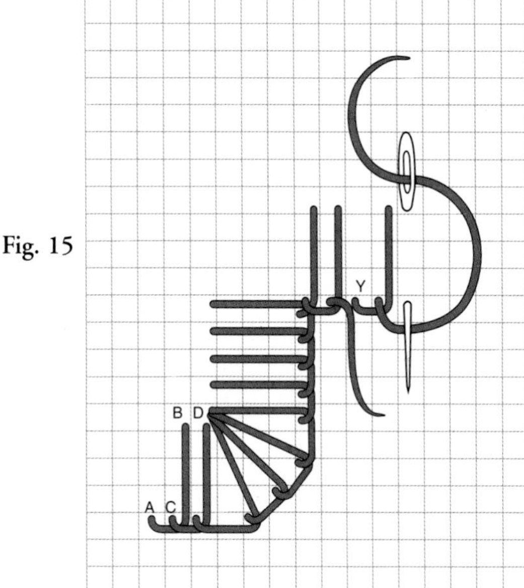

7 When you have finished the working thread, return to the loose thread at the join and 'missing' stitch. Take this thread under the small beginning loop of the working thread at Y and down into the fabric at Z (Fig. 16). Fasten off at the back of the work.

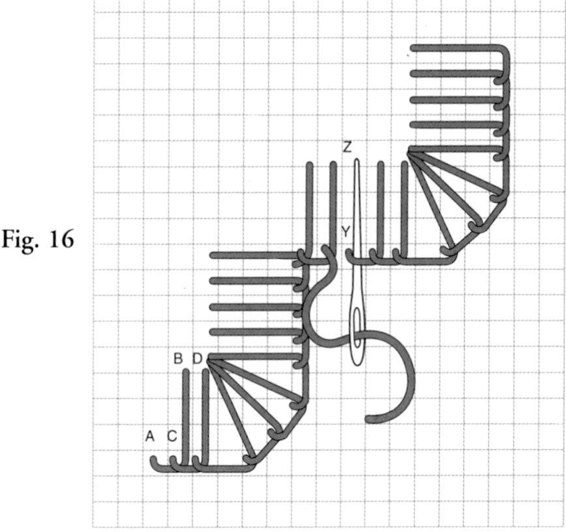

Fig. 16

8 Complete the embroidery, wash and press before cutting the fabric away from buttonhole stitch.

9 Carefully cut the fabric thread from the back of the work in case one or two buttonhole stitches are not correctly positioned. Try not to cut the buttonhole loops on the right side. (It is not the end of the world if you do, just a nuisance to unravel the cut thread and redo the buttonhole edging.)

Twisted Lattice Band (Kjederand)

This decorative stitch (Fig. 17) gives the appearance of a delicate braid and is often used to border the collars and cuffs of shirts worn with the Hardanger 'bunad'.

1 To form the cross stitches, work a row of diagonal stitches from right to left over four threads, returning in the opposite direction.

2 The surface lacing is woven in two journeys on top of the crossed stitches as shown, working from right to left for the bottom row and in the opposite direction for the top row.

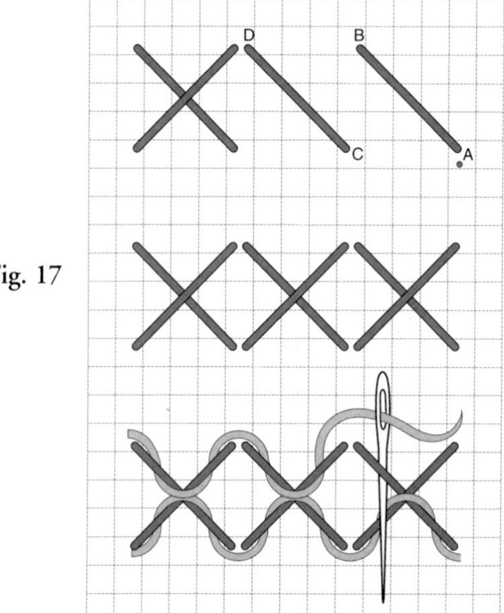

Fig. 17

Hem Stitch (Holsaum)

Hemstitching (a drawn-thread technique) is a decorative way of securing a hem on evenweave fabric, or bordering garments and household linen (Figs. 18-21).

1 Using sharp scissors, cut through the number of horizontal threads to be withdrawn, 10cm (4in) from either edge (Fig. 18). Carefully withdraw the threads to the edge, holding the fabric tightly at the sides to prevent the threads from pulling further than necessary.

Fig. 18

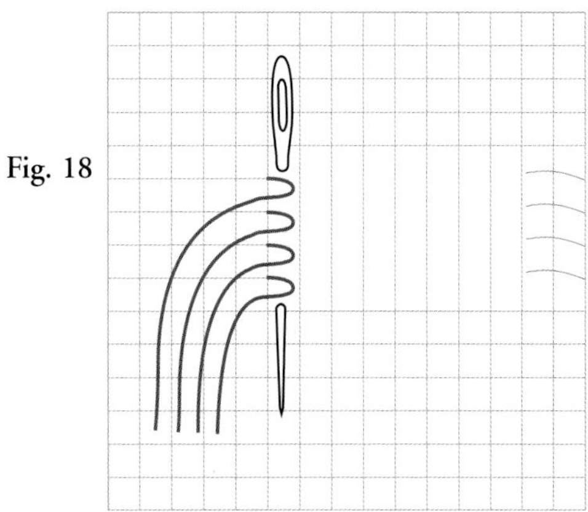

2 To secure, take the ends to the back of the fabric. Thread each end separately, follow the weave of the fabric and darn the threads in for about 2cm (¾in) (Fig. 19) or stitch down with back stitch.

Fig. 19

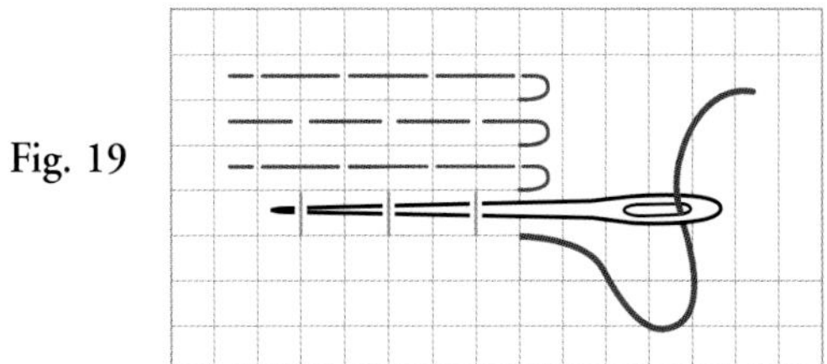

3 To work the hem stitch, working from left to right, secure a thread, and bring the needle to the front, two threads beneath the edge of the drawn threads at A (Fig. 20).

Fig. 20

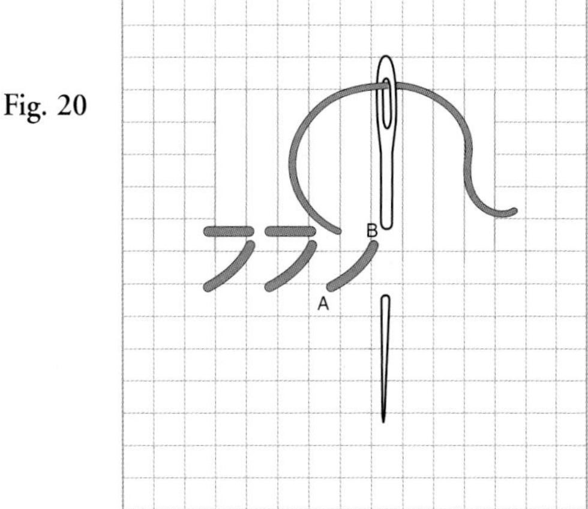

4 Take the thread across the front from left to right and pick up the first two vertical threads as shown.

5 Wrap the threads and pull tightly, inserting the needle as shown, and surfacing just to the right of the worked threads at B.

6 Repeat along the row, fastening off the thread as neatly as possible.

7 To work an opposite second row, turn the work round and repeat, grouping the stitches to form clusters exactly opposite each other (Fig. 21).

Fig. 21

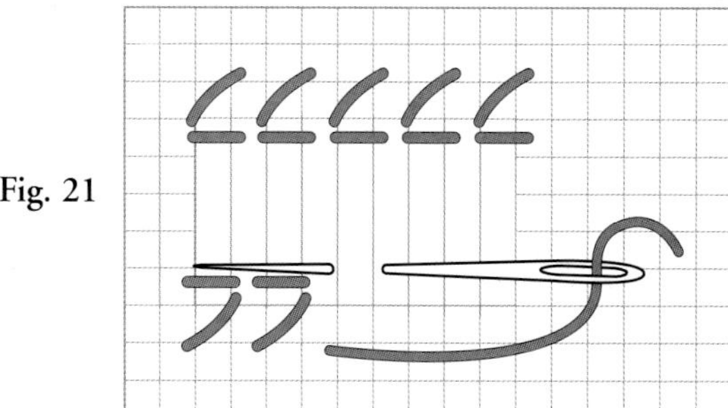

SURFACE EMBROIDERY

Exciting, rich effects can be achieved easily with the knowledge of just a few simple embroidery stitches – which could develop into a lifetime passion for working with threads and fabrics. Delicate and textured stitchery using fine silk or stranded cotton (floss) will give your work individuality, and beads can add yet another dimension to your treasured heirlooms. New threads are constantly becoming available. Space-dyed threads, shimmering silks and rayons, fine cottons, glittering iridescent and metallic threads, and interestingly textured yarns make this seductive world of colour and texture irresistible to an embroiderer.

Fabrics

The surface embroidery projects in this book have silk, cotton or fine wool backgrounds, as I love to work with natural fibres. If you prefer to work on a different backing, choose a fabric appropriate to the type of project and one which will be able to support the embroidery.

Threads

I have embroidered with either single strands of medium-thickness silk thread, or stranded cotton (floss). If you have a preferred alternative thread, work a small sample on your background fabric to make sure it will achieve the right effect and that it will lie on the fabric without puckering. If you choose to put silk thread on a project that might be washed, check before you start that the thread is colour fast and washable. The thickness of your thread will determine the final result; use fine threads for delicacy, thicker threads for weight and boldness. Always 'strip' stranded cotton (floss) before using it (see page 9). Use an organiser to keep all threads in good order (see page 8). Each project has instructions regarding which needle to use.

Using a hoop

Use a small embroidery hoop approximately 10-15cm (4-6in), and bind the inner ring with 25mm (1in) cotton tape.

When working on silk and very fine cotton, I bind both rings of my hoop with tape and put a strip of cotton on the edge of the fabric when positioning the hoop to prevent marking or distorting the fabric. Try to keep the fabric straight when putting it in the hoop, and keep your work fairly taut to make stitching easier and prevent puckering. Always remove the hoop when you have finished working.

Transferring the design

Each project has instructions for transferring the design. The method employed is generally governed by the type of fabric, design and colour. For marking the design use a Quilter's Ultimate marking pencil or No. 2 pencil. Always test for washing. Never use a marker that does not wash out.

Starting and finishing

To start, bring your thread to the surface and work a couple of back stitches on top of each other to secure the thread where it will be covered by embroidery. Or, start with a small knot on the back a short distance away from your first stitch. Work over the thread towards the knot to secure the thread and cut off the knot when you reach it.

To finish, work a few back stitches on top of each other and weave your thread through the backs of several completed stitches.

Keeping your work clean

Silk fabric is expensive, so if you are going to use it for your background, work on a white cloth or apron and wash your hands frequently. Keep your work in a pillow case.

If your project does need washing when it is completed, check first that all materials are washable. Then hand wash using a mild soap powder, wrap in a towel and dry flat. Press lightly from the back onto a soft cloth.

Surface Embroiderey Stitches

French Knot

French knots (Figs. 1-2) can be used densely for filling, or singly to add texture or a speck of colour.

Fig. 1

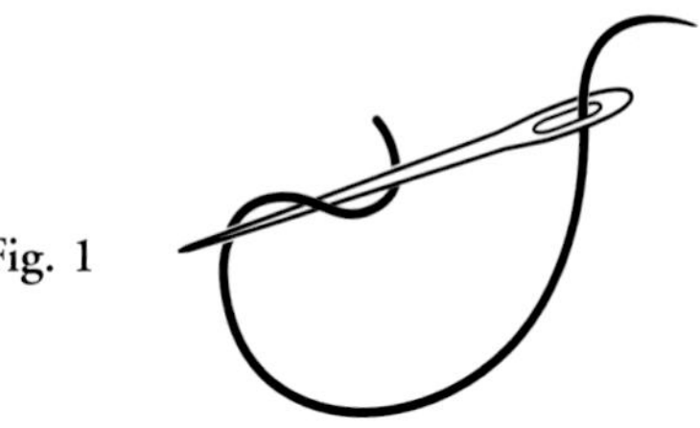

Fig. 2

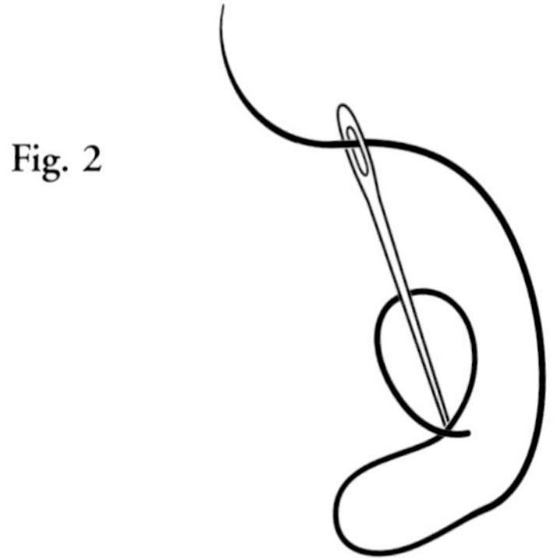

1 Bring the needle up through the fabric to the front.

2 Holding the thread tightly in one hand, twist the needle away from you, round the thread.

3 Pull up the twist, turn the needle and stab back into the fabric near the initial entry, pushing the needle and thread through the knot.

Detached Chain

This much used and loved stitch (Fig. 3) can be worked on its own, or in groups to form flower or leaf shapes (join five or six to make petals for a small daisy head).

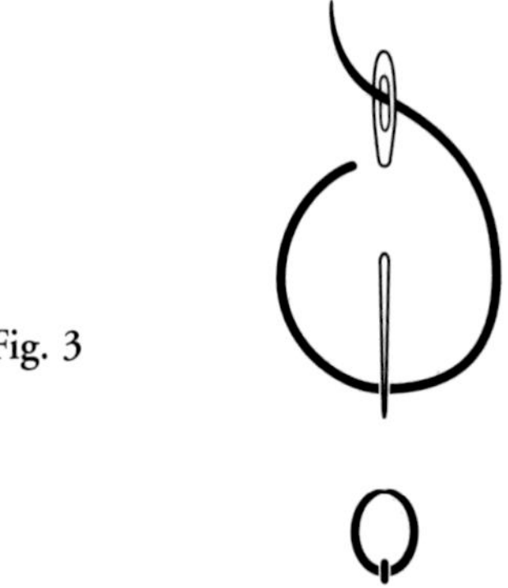

Fig. 3

1 Bring the needle through to the surface.

2 Insert the needle near the initial entry, looping the thread underneath as shown.

3 Where you come to the surface determines the stitch size. Pull the needle through the loop. Secure with a small vertical stitch.

4 Position the next stitch where required.

Stem Stitch

This outline stitch (Fig. 4) can be used to work any awkward curves and shapes. With the thread to the right of the needle, make small even stitches as shown.

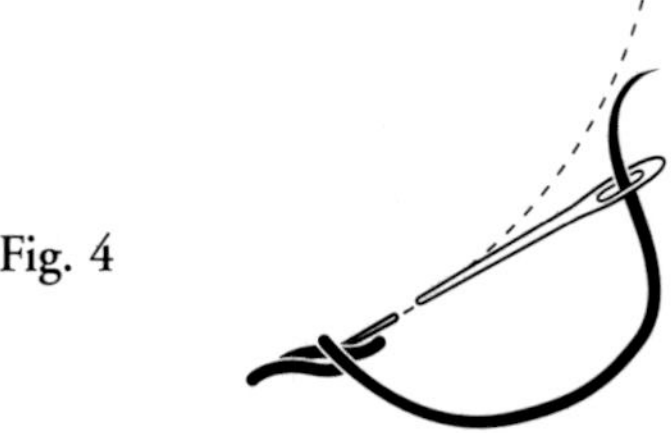

Fig. 4

Fly Stitch

Quick and easy to work, this stitch combines well with others.

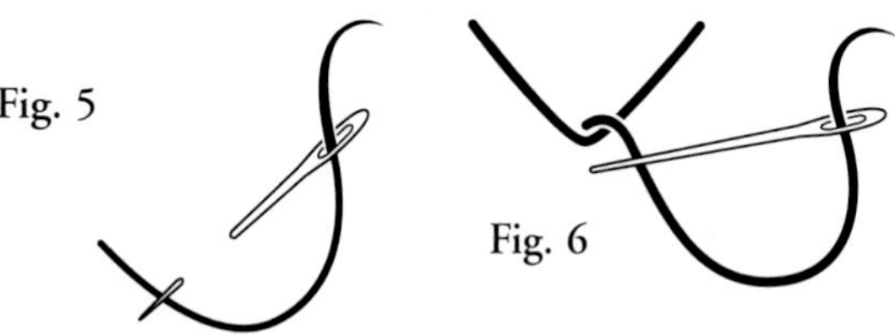

Fig. 5

Fig. 6

1 Bring the needle through to the front of the fabric, then take a diagonal stitch with the thread under the needle to form a Y loop.

2 Hold the loop in position with a small vertical straight stitch.

Bullion Knot

Wrapped thread forms this long textured knotted stitch (Figs. 7-9) which can be used to make flowers. The number of wraps will vary according to the thickness of the thread and the effect required.

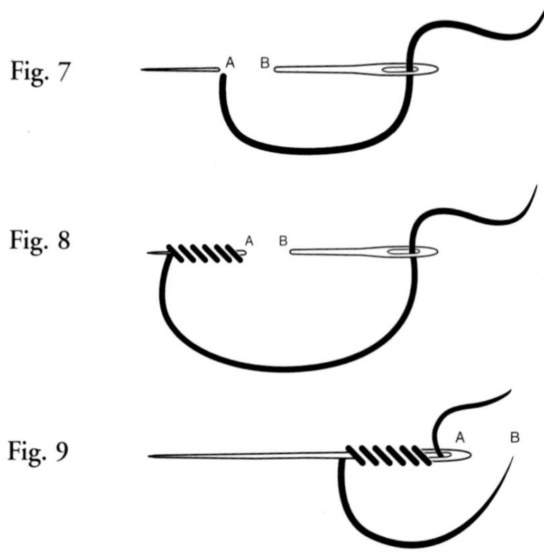

Fig. 7

Fig. 8

Fig. 9

1 Bring the needle through to the front of the fabric at A.

2 Insert it at B a short distance away then bring it back up at A.

3 With the needle in this position, wrap the thread around it seven or eight times.

4 Tighten the coiled thread until the coils are even, and, holding the thread securely with one hand, pull the needle and thread through the coils. If necessary, adjust and tighten the thread so that the bullion knot is perfectly formed on the surface of the fabric.

5 Take the needle back down through the fabric at B to anchor the knot.

Bullion Bud

Bullion knots can be straight or curved to represent flower shapes.

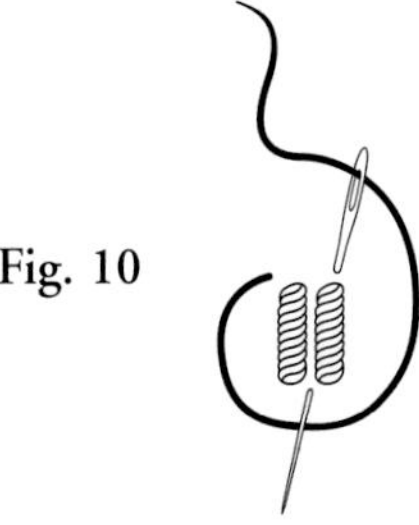

Fig. 10

1 Make two bullion knots close together

2 Outline with a single fly stitch to form a bud.

Bullion Rose

Curved bullion knots are particularly effective as 'petals' of a rose.

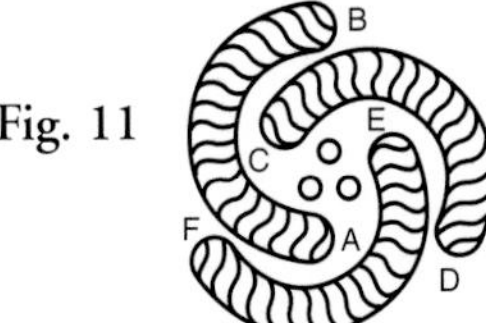

Fig. 11

1 Work the bullion rose round three central French knots.

2 Follow Fig. 11 showing the order of work and keep building up the petals to form the shape required.

Ladder Stitch

This invaluable stitch (Figs. 12-13) gives invisible seam joins.

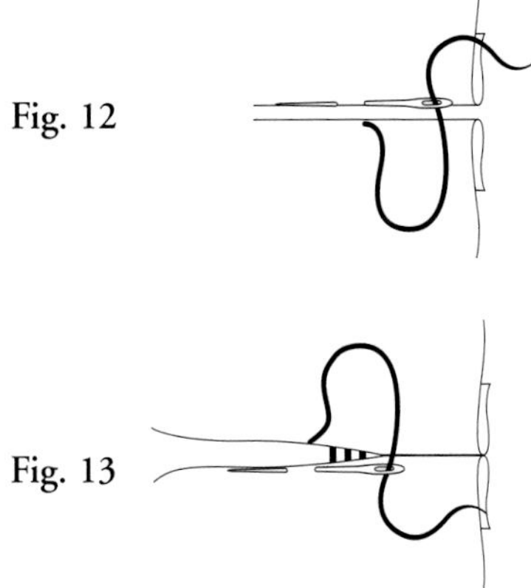

Fig. 12

Fig. 13

1 Butt the two edges of fabric to be joined.

2 Secure the thread, take the needle from one edge and insert in the other edge opposite.

3 Make a small horizontal stitch and repeat.

4 Work four small stitches before pulling up the thread to bring the edges close together.

Sewing on a Bead

1 Bring a fine or beading needle to the front of the fabric, thread on a bead and take a small stitch back into the fabric.

2 If you have a lot of single beads to sew on, make several small back stitches after every third bead to secure.

CHAPTER 2

WEDDINGS

This chapter celebrates that all important wedding day. A hundred and one memories make up this momentous occasion but the projects which follow will provide tangible reminders. Four different embroidery techniques are used for the projects which include:

A pair of 'kneeler' cushions in canvas work which will last a lifetime.

A cross stich wedding sampler which combined with photographs will record the event and take pride of place.

A small bridal bag embroidered with rich surface stitchery which will serve as a constant reminder of the wedding dress.

A herb pillow in heirloom sewing which is both practical and decorative.

'Wedding Rings' Canvas Work Kneeler Cushions

The wedding ring, symbolizing everlasting love and commitment, is the theme of this continuous design for a pair of initialled kneeler cushions. After the wedding couple has used them at the altar, the cushions will brighten up a new home and be a constant reminder of a joyous occasion. The project incorporates simple canvas work stitches in traditional bridal colours of pastel yellow, white and green. Crewel wool, stranded cotton and silk ribbon combine to give these cushions a soft glow of their own and make them a present to value for always.The cushions have a mitred silk-fabric border and cord edging, but there is fabric allowance for piping if preferred.

Size of canvas design: *30.5cm (12in) square*
Size of finished cushion: *43cm (17in) square*

Materials (each cushion)

0.5m (19in) square white mono de-luxe canvas, 18 threads to the inch

1oz hank Appleton crewel wool 871, 872

2 x 1oz hanks Appleton crewel wool 991b

4 skeins Anchor stranded cotton (floss) 292 (yellow)

2 skeins Anchor stranded cotton (floss) 259, 260 (green)

Tapestry needles size 22 (for the crewel wool), and 24 (for the ribbon and stranded cotton/floss)

5m (5½yd) pale-yellow silk ribbon, 2mm (approximately ⅛in) wide

2.5m (2¾yd) white cotton tape, 25mm (1in) wide

2.5m (2¾yd) twisted cord for edging

46cm (18in) cushion pad

0.7m (¾yd) yellow silk fabric, plus thread to match

0.7m (¾yd) lining fabric

61cm (24in) roller frame or 46cm (18in) square wooden frame/artist's canvas stretcher bars

Drawing pins or staple gun

Instructions

1 Read and refer to the section on basic canvas work techniques and stitches, pages 8-19. Prepare the canvas, tack (baste) the centre lines and attach it to the frame.

2 Referring to the key for threads and numbers of strands to use, start stitching 13.5cm (5⅜in) from the centre point at A. Following the chart, work the straight-gobelin-star motifs anticlockwise in crewel wool. Keep

checking that they are lined up opposite each other (in both directions). Then stitch the linking half stars. Leave the diagonal stitches 1b, 2b, 3b and 4b, to be completed at the end using the silk ribbon.

3 Fill the diamonds (1) formed by the star motifs with Alicia's lace, using two strands of each of the green stranded cottons (floss).

4 Using tent stitch and four strands of yellow stranded cotton, fill the small linking squares (2) between the points of the star motifs. Outline each square with a back stitch over one thread to cover the canvas and neaten the edges. As you work from square to square, highlight the half-star motifs (3) by covering the diagonal stitch previously worked in crewel wool.

5 Stitch an upright cross stitch in the centre of the tent-stitch square.

6 Keeping the colours correct, complete the outline of the central medallion.

7 Choose your initial from the alphabet on pages 52-53 and centre it in the medallion. Stitch the initial in rice stitch in green stranded cotton (floss). Following the key and the chart, fill the inner spaces of the initial with tent stitch in yellow wool and the medallion background with Alicia's lace in white wool.

8 Hungarian stitch (4) is used for the background, changing direction in different parts of the design (see the chart).

9 On the outside edges of the canvas, the Hungarian stitch background is mitred at the corners (see chart). Stitch each section

to the corner and turn the work a quarter turn. You will now be able to work as before and the design will mitre at the corner.

10 Work the border at the edges of the canvas in straight gobelin stitch over four threads, mitred at the corners. Add a further line of tent stitch outside the border to prevent the canvas showing in case the machine stitching line is not quite straight when you make up the cushion.

11 Finally, using silk ribbon, stitch the diagonals 1b, 2b, 3b and 4b on all the straight gobelin stars. Refer to starting and finishing with ribbon on page 11, and keep the ribbon as flat as possible.

12 Stretch the canvas back into shape (page 11).

Making up the Cushion

1 Measure the length of each side of the stitched canvas, adding 18cm (7in) to each length. Cut four strips of silk and lining fabric to this length by 9cm (3½in) wide.

2 Place one strip along one edge of the canvas (1.3cm/½in seam), right sides together and centred. Machine against the edge of the canvas, finishing at the corners of the design (Fig. 1). Repeat on the other three sides.

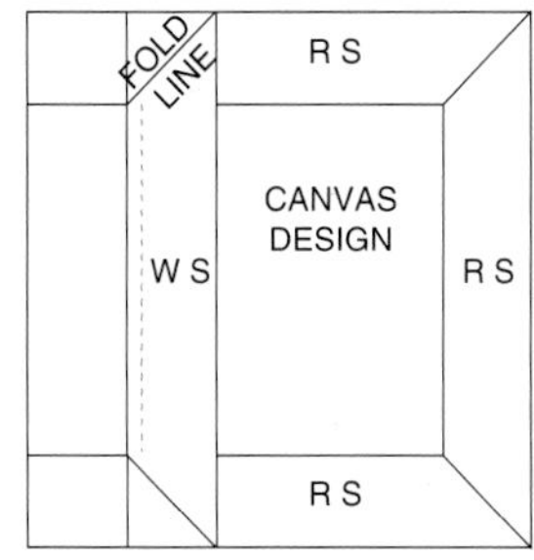

Fig. 1

3 Mark the mitres by folding the fabric under at a right angle at each corner, and pressing the diagonal line. Tack (baste) along each mitre and machine stitch or ladderstitch together. Trim excess fabric and press seams open.

4 Cut the back fabric to the same size as the front and place right sides together. Machine stitch the seams, leaving an opening large enough to take the pad.

5 Place pad in cover, pushing out the corners. Ladderstitch the opening (see page 37).

6 Stitch the cord in place round the edges (Fig. 2), working a slanting stitch following the twist. At each corner make an overhand knot and small loop. To join up whip each end of the cord to prevent fraying and at the last corner lose the ends in the overhand knot at the back. Secure with stitching.

Fig. 2

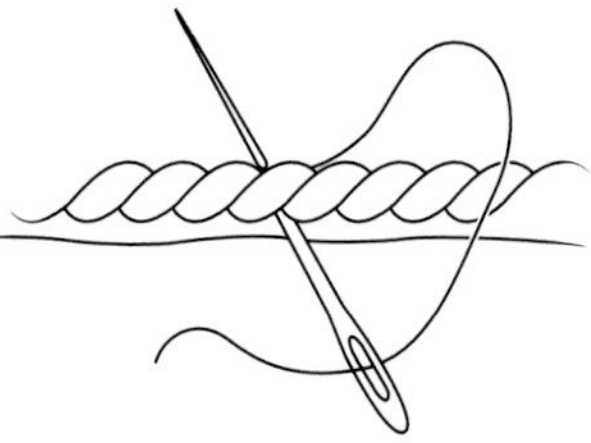

Alternative ideas and suggestions

- Change the colourway to match the fabric of the bride's, or the bridesmaids' dresses.
- Sew a small pearl or matching bead into the centre of the stars.

B
J

KEY

Each grid line represents one thread of fabric.

Straight gobelin star
Appleton 871
3 strands

Half gobelin star
Appleton 872
3 strands

Alicia's Lace
Anchor 259 & 260
2 strands of each

Alicia's Lace
Appleton 991b
2 strands

Tent stitch & back
Anchor 292
4 strands

Upright cross
Appleton 872
2 strands

Hungarian stitch
Appleton 991b
3 strands

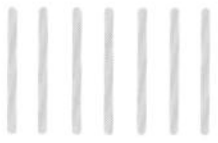

Straight gobelin
Appleton 873
3 strands

Rice stitch
Anchor 259 & 260
2 strands of each

Tent stitch
Appleton 873
2 strands

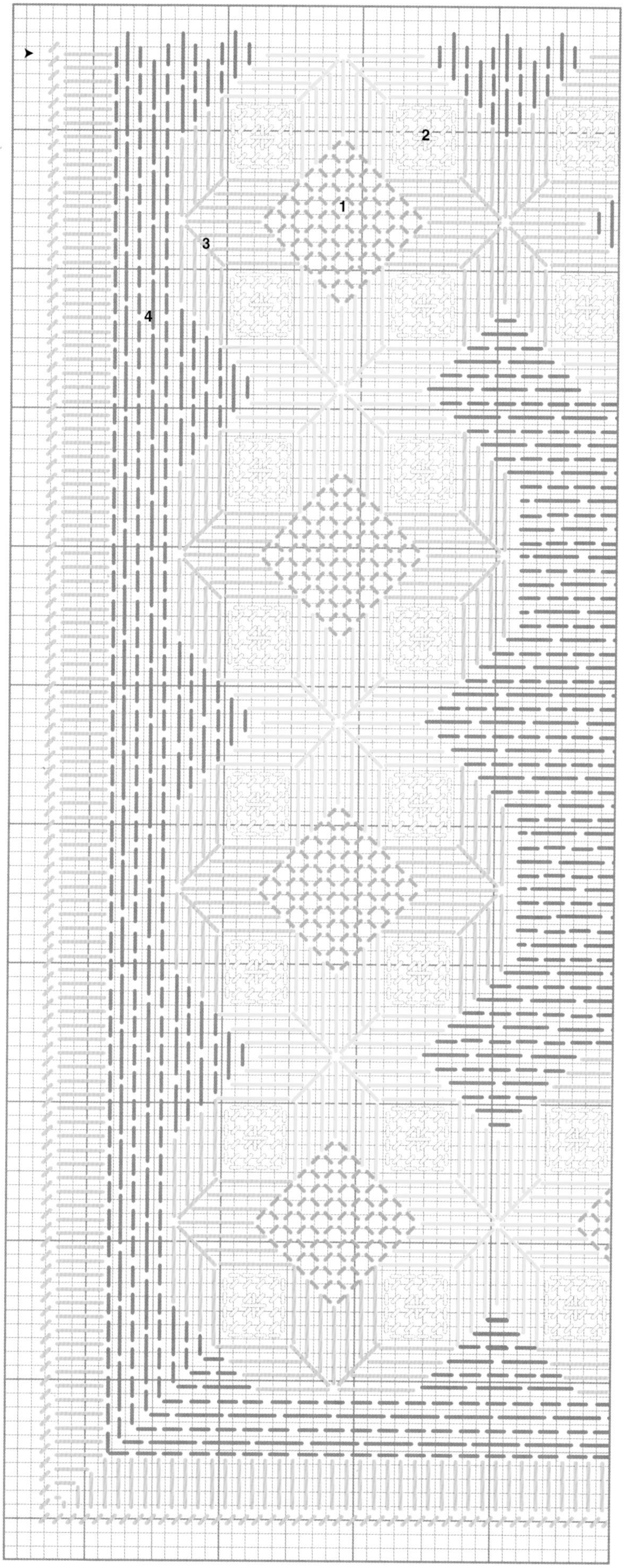

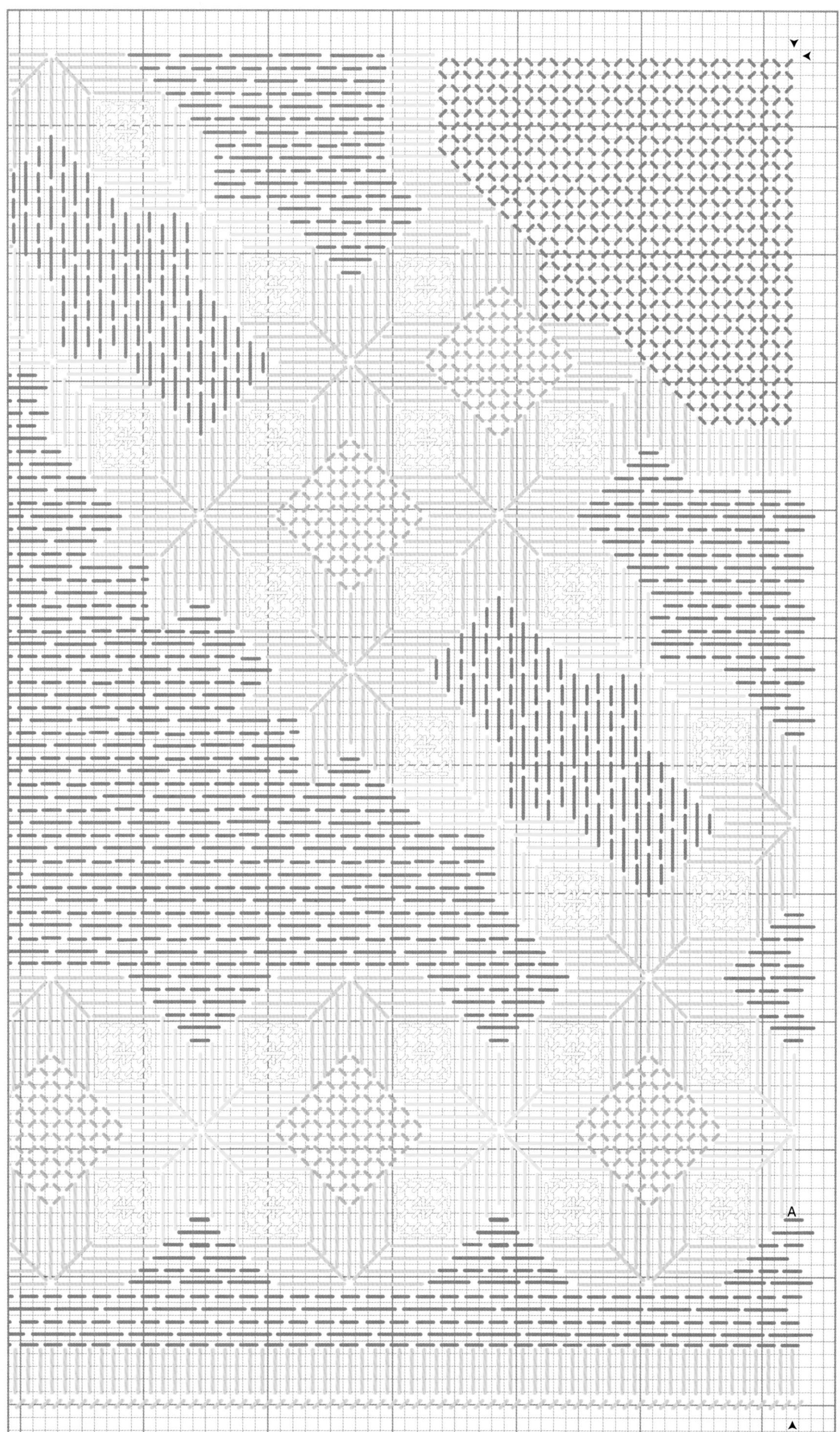
A

'Memories' Triptych Sampler in Cross Stitch

This is a triptych with a difference, evoking memories of a special occasion. The design worked in simple cross stitch on linen has a border of ivy and violets surrounding the Church, to symbolise steadfastness, friendship and fidelity. The humble proverb 'Love begets love' imparts an appropriate message. Easily completed when time is limited, this sampler could also be worked to celebrate other important milestones such as anniversaries, and it could be used alone, without the side panels. The date and initials (and photographs, if used) will identify the event being commemorated. Alternatively, the initials could be replaced with small relevant spot motifs.

Finished size of central panel: *32 x 22cm (12⅝ x 8⅝in)*

Materials

46 x 36cm (18 x 14in) white evenweave linen, 26 threads to the inch

1 skein each Anchor stranded cotton (floss): 883, 884, 392, 852, 235, 1041, 278, 267, 268, 118, 119, 260, 262

10cm (4in) embroidery hoop

Tapestry needle size 24

Instructions

1 Prepare the linen following the instructions on page 25. Read and refer to the section on canvas work (which deals with necessary basic techniques even though you are working on linen). Group and organize the threads. Place the linen in the embroidery hoop but always remember to release it if you leave the embroidery for any length of time.

2 Start stitching with an away knot. This design is worked in cross stitch over a single thread using one strand. I prefer to complete each stitch as I go, but there are other ways of working cross stitch all of which are acceptable. Whichever way you prefer, it is essential that the top stitches all lie in the same direction to present a smooth and even finish. When finishing threads, weave carefully through the back of previously worked stitches, adding the occasional back stitch for security. Try not to take thread across the back from area to area in case it shows up as a dark line.

3 Following the chart and the key, start with the outline and basic shape of the church. Count from the centre square. Complete the roof, the windows and the door.

4 Work the flints on the main part of the church as follows. Using thread 852, randomly spot single cross stitches in each section. Refer to the colour photograph if it helps. Change to thread 392 and repeat the random spotting as before, sometimes working one or two stitches together round the first spot to create a small pale area. Finally fill in with colour 235. If necessary, add more pale flecks as you work.

5 Finish the rest of the design following the chart and key and adding lettering from the alphabet on pages 52-53. If your date has fewer letters, you could add an extra leaf on either side.

6 When complete, hand wash the sampler, if necessary, using a mild soap powder. Dry face down on towelling, stretch carefully back into shape and press when damp.

Lacing your embroidery

1 Use a piece of cardboard that has been cut to the required size, preferably acid-free (available from art shops or picture framers).

2 Outline tack the finished size of the embroidery on your fabric, following the straight grain.

3 With the embroidery right side down on to a clean surface, line up the card on the tacked outline on the back.

4 Position with pins inserted into the edge of the card.

5 Using a length of strong thread sufficient to complete a side, lace across the back, working from the centre outwards (Fig. 1). Pull the thread tightly. Complete the other side.

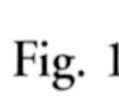
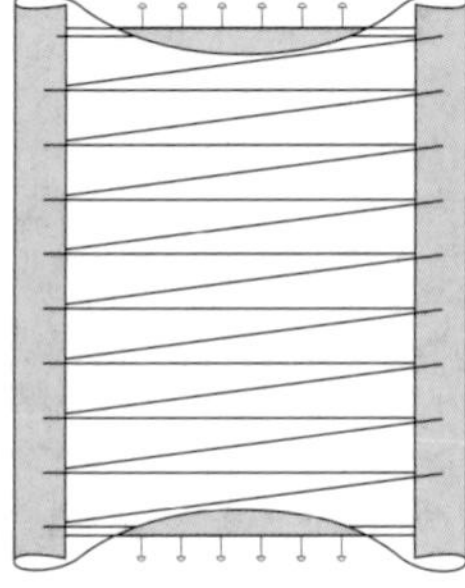

Fig. 1

6 Repeat in the other direction, lacing under and over the first line of threads, again working from the centre to the sides (Fig. 2).

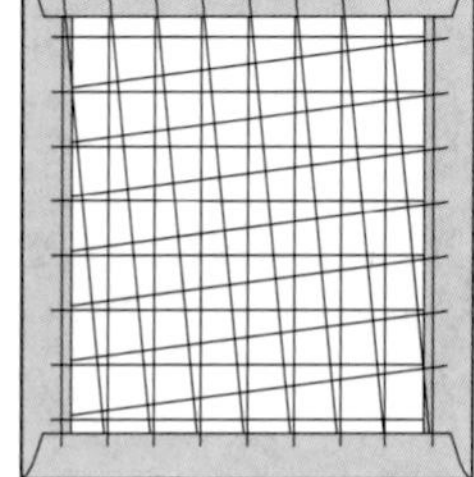

Fig. 2

7 Check continuously that the front is still straight, and adjust if necessary.

8 Fold over the corners and complete the lacing right to the edges (Fig. 2).

9 Cover the lacing with a piece of fabric hemmed into position.

10 Take the sampler to a professional picture framer to make up into the triptych. Choose a neutral-coloured mount and simple moulding which will not detract from the embroidery.

17th December 1940
BP
UG
Love begets Love

KEY

Each square represents one cross stitch over a single thread. Use one strand for each stitch.

Church

● Outline Anchor 883

○ Roof Anchor 884, 883

✖ Windows Anchor 1041

Flints and background (unmarked on chart) Anchor 852, 235, 392

Ivy

/ Outside of leaves Anchor 278

\ Inside of leaves Anchor 267

● Stems Anchor 268

Violets

● Light shading Anchor 118

● Dark shading Anchor 119

/ Stems Anchor 260

✕ Leaves Anchor 262

× Flower centre (French knot) Anchor 1041

Bushes

× Stem Anchor 268

\ Leaves Anchor 267

— Grass Anchor 262

Lettering

× Date Anchor 883

○ Proverb (1st letter) Anchor 884

× (remainder) Anchor 883

Initials

× 1st letter Anchor 119

× 2nd letter Anchor 118

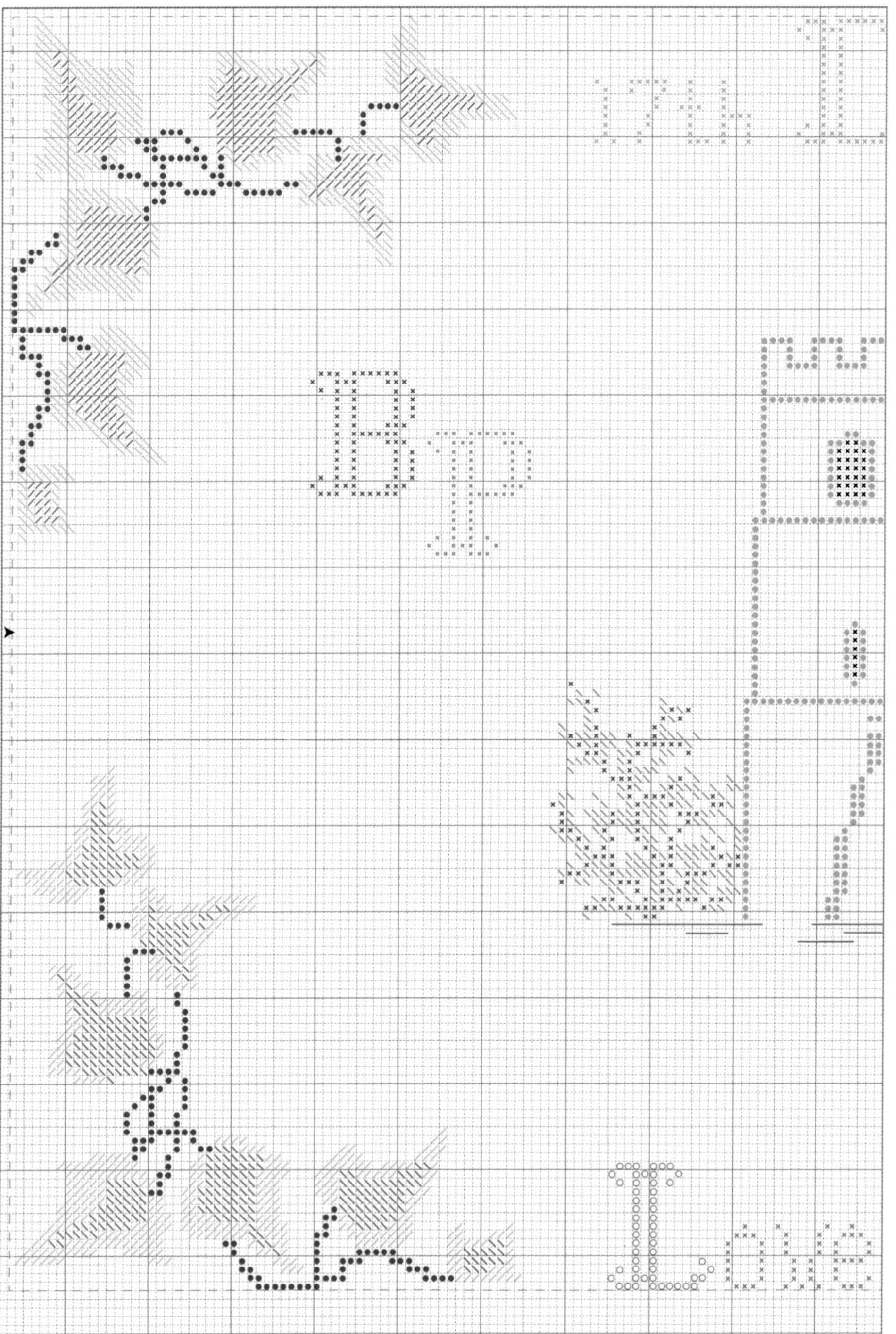

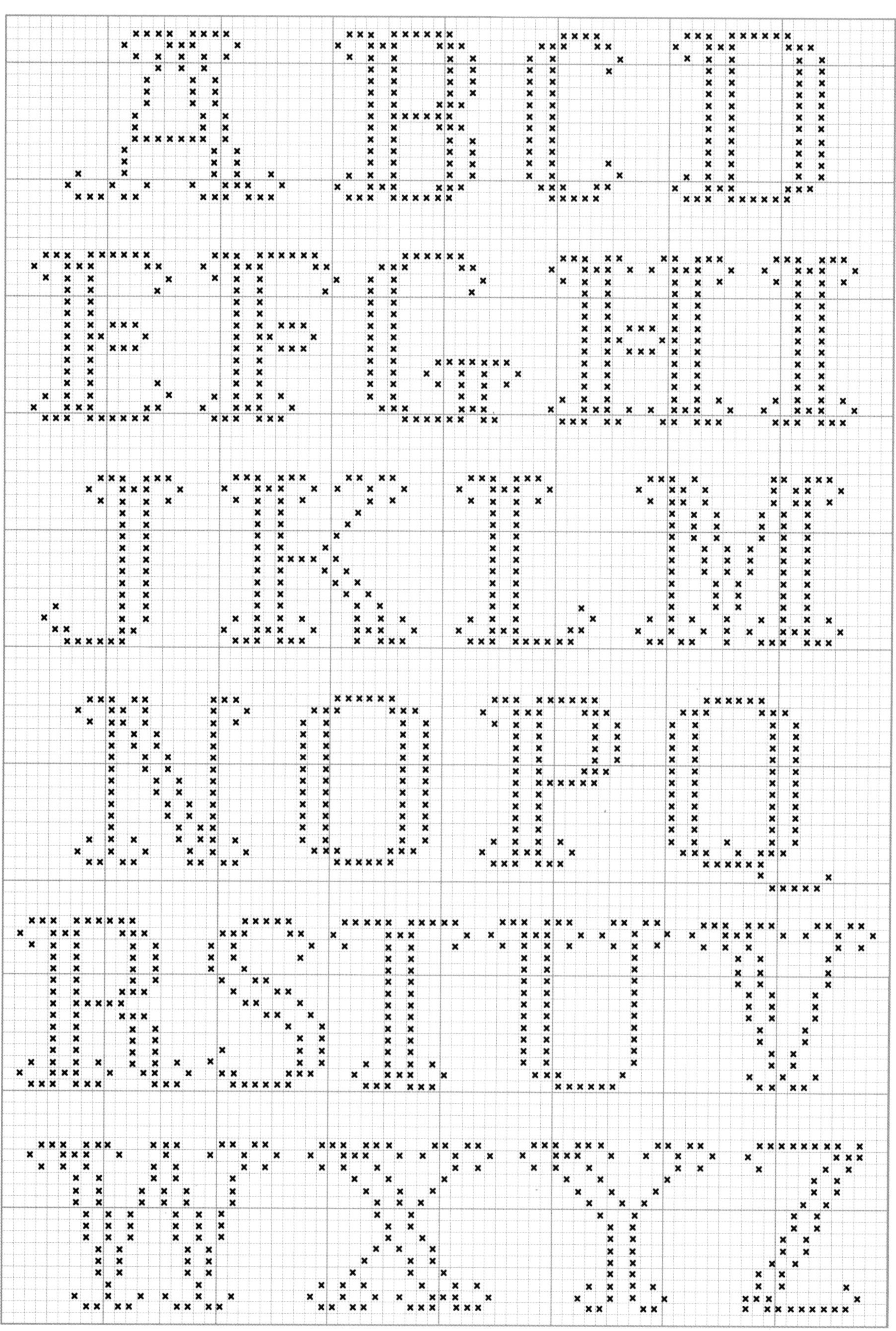

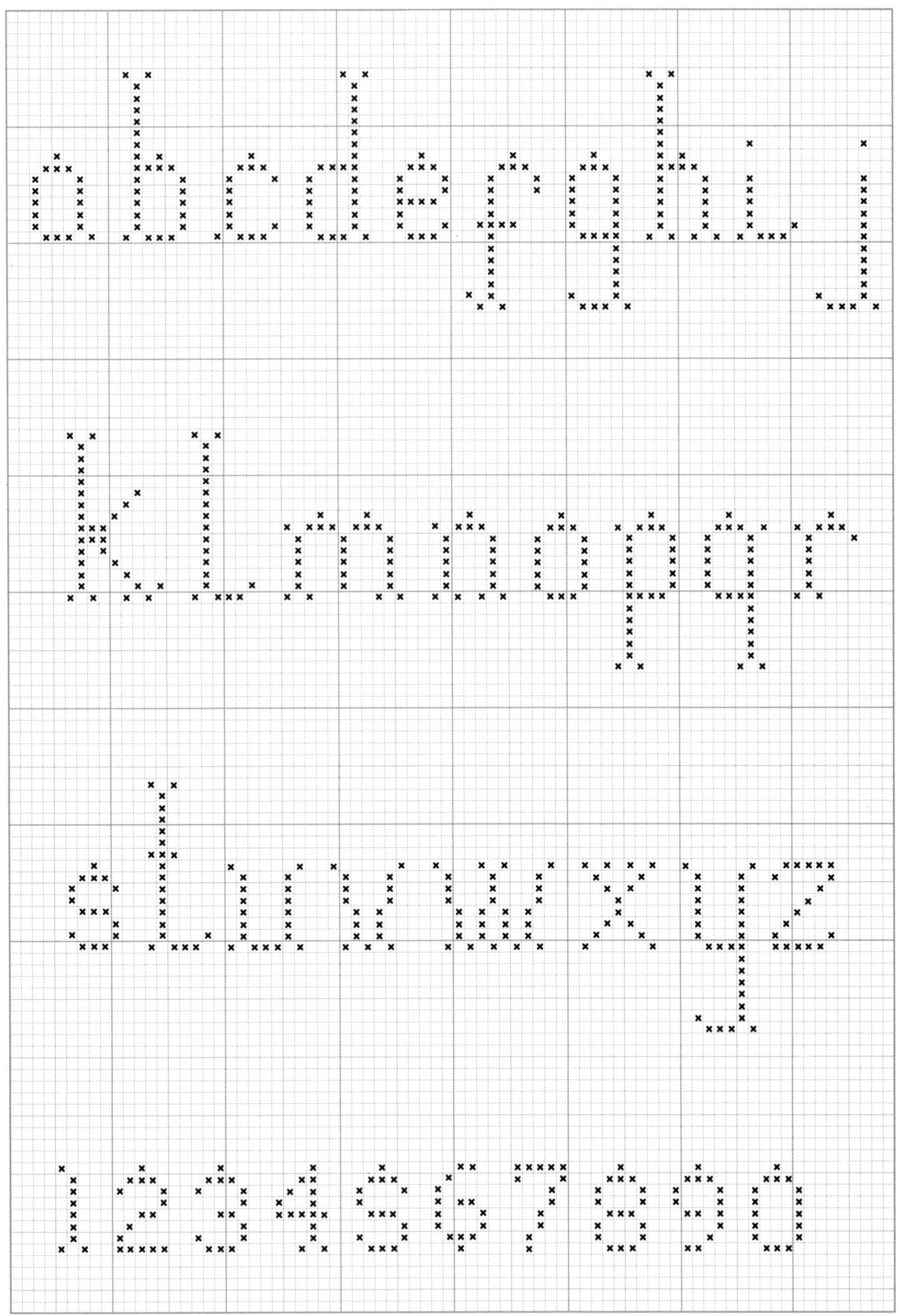

'Bags of Happiness' Bridal Bag With Surface Embroiderery

This unique folded bag is delicately embroidered with a simple design of roses and forget-me-nots, which uses just a few surface embroidery stitches. The small flaps show off the embroidery to perfection and hide secret pockets. Tassels add just a touch of flamboyance. After the big occasion, it can continue to be enjoyed as a handkerchief or jewel case.

The embroidery has been stitched in Mulberry silks, but Anchor stranded cotton (floss) equivalents are given in brackets as an alternative.

Finished size: *19 x 23cm (7½ x 9in)*

Materials

56cm (22in) square of silk dupion, or fabric to match the bride's dress

56cm (22in) square of the same fabric for the lining

56cm (22in) square of silk organza (interlining)

36cm (14in) fine bias piping or twisted cord (optional)

Few pearl beads (optional)

Mulberry Silks thread (medium) 1 of each

Roses: Yellows – dark No. S327, medium No. S326, pale No. S325

Buds, leaves and stalk: Greens No. S282, S283

Forget-me-nots: Blue No. R143

(or Anchor Stranded Cotton: Yellows No. 295, 293, 292; Greens No. 264, 265; Blue No. 144)

Crewel needle size 9

Straw needle size 9 (for bullions)

Small embroidery hoop

Pastel-coloured tacking (basting) cotton

1m (39in) twisted cord (purchased or hand made)

4 small ceramic beads for cord and tassels

Pastel or silver fabric marking pencil

Hard pencil

Tissue paper

Paper

Instructions

1 Read and refer to the section on surface embroiderery techniques and stitches, pages 34-37.

2 Tack (baste) the interlining to the back of the top fabric using long stitches in lines 16cm (6in) apart. Oversew the edges to prevent fraying.

3 Trace and cut a paper pattern from the template below. Transfer all the guidelines.

4 Practise folding your paper template before folding the fabric (Fig. 1). Fold the corner 2 over to intersection Y. Take the corner 4 across to intersection Z. Fold the corner flaps 1 and 3 down into the triangle formed by the crossed corners. Finger crease these lines (Fig. 2). Fold this rectangular shape in half, back on itself, along the line 2-Z-Y-4, with the flaps facing outwards. This gives the basic shape of the bag (Fig. 3).

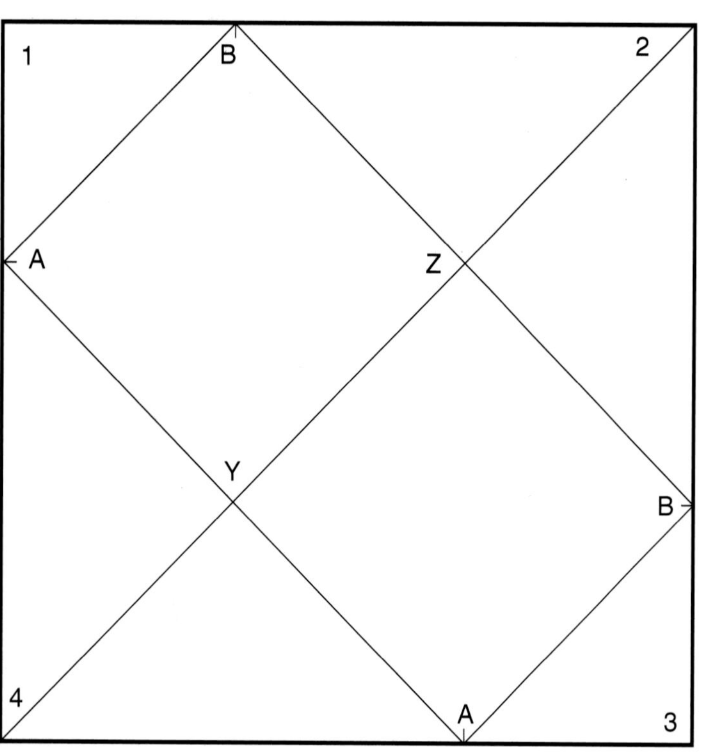

Fig. 1

Bridal bag template

Final measurement is 48cm (19in) square. The template above is 20% of actual size so please enlarge on a photocopier by 500%.

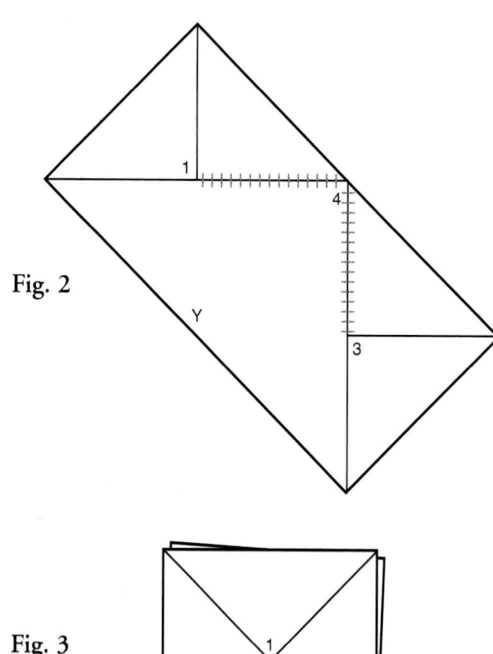

Fig. 2

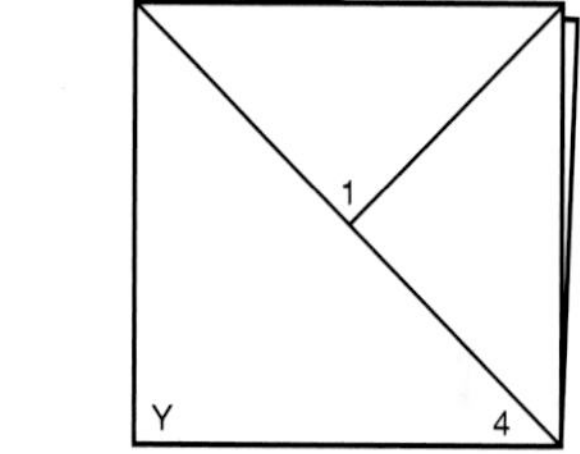

Fig. 3

5 Using a hard pencil, trace two copies of the floral design (page 59) on to tissue paper, plus the two right-angled guide lines and the broken line to help centre the design.

6 Centre the template (open) on the fabric square, carefully marking and then tacking (basting) round the outline. Do not cut off the excess fabric.

7 Position the guide lines of your traced design on the tacking (basting) line in corner 1 on the right side of the fabric. Outline tack (baste) the shape of the stems and buds, the position of leaves, and the broken straight line marking the centre of the design. Mark the centres of the roses with two small dots, and the centres of the forget-me-nots with one dot. Carefully tear the tissue paper away, leaving the tacking stitches. Repeat on the opposite corner 3.

8 Place the fabric in the hoop. Following the key, embroider the bullion roses, then the stem-stitch branches, the buds, the leaves and lastly the forget-me-nots.

Constructing the bag

1 If you are using bias piping, attach it at this stage round corners 1 and 3, on the tacking (basting) outline.Take the piping to the flap fold and lose ends into the seam as shown at A and B in Fig. 4. Machine into position. If you choose to use cord, it can be attached once the bag is completed.

Fig. 4

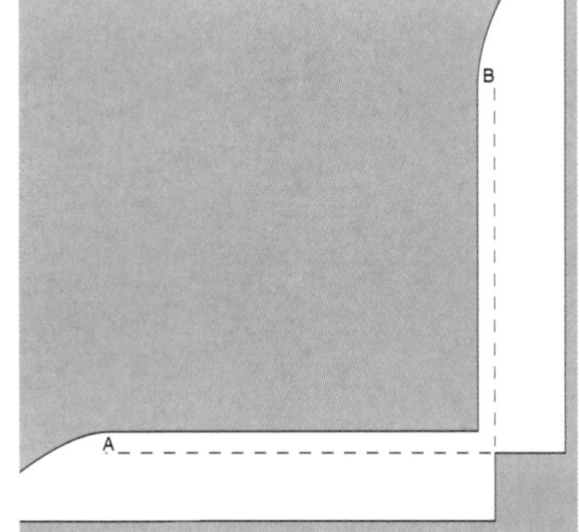

2 Place the lining and embroidered fabric right sides together. Machine stitch along the tacked (basted) outline leaving a 10cm (4in) opening near an unembroidered corner.

3 Trim excess fabric, turn inside out and press. Ladderstitch (page 37) the opening.

4 Re-position the template over the completed square to mark points A and B with pins. Tack (baste) in the fold lines AB, AYA, BZB and YZ and fold fabric as practised on the template.

5 Ladderstitch the crossed-over corner edges (2) to join the fabric as shown in Fig. 2. Repeat on the inside of the bag.

6 Fold in half along the line 2-Z-Y-4 and ladderstitch up the sides of the bag from the bottom fold, ending 3.5cm (1⅜in) from the top.

7 To form a casing for the cords, hold the 'envelope' flaps and gently pull down level with the line of completed ladder stitch.

Machine stitch a line 12mm (½in) from the top and a second line 25mm (1in) from the top.

8 Thread the desired length of cord through the casing, wrap the ends tightly together and finish off with beads and tassels. Backstitch small pearl beads along the front seams and onto the edge of the flap.

Making the tassel

Used singly or grouped, tassels are an excellent and exotic finishing touch. They can be attached as a specific detail, grouped for effect or added just for fun. Use fibres which hang well, and do not be afraid to mix colours and textures of yarns. Different thicknesses produce different effects.

1 Wind the required number of threads round a piece of card which you cut to the length of the tassel needed (Fig. 5).

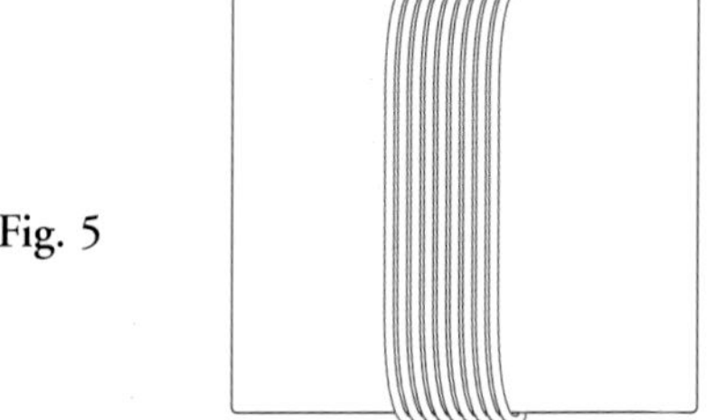

Fig. 5

2 Gather up the top of the loops onto a cord or length of thread. slide the card through the loops or cut through the bottom of the loops to release (Fig. 6).

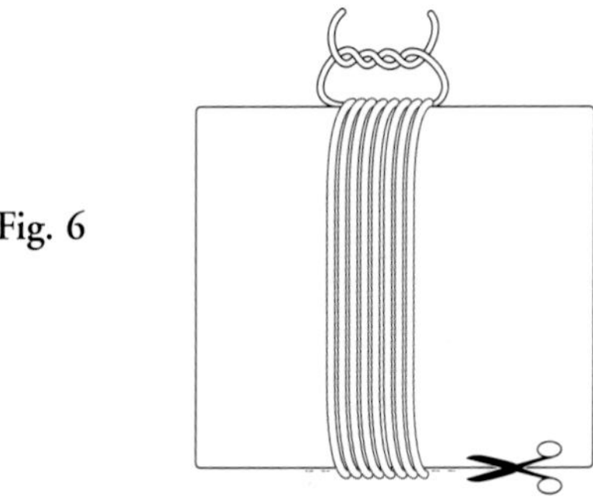

Fig. 6

3 Bind the tassel about 12mm (½in) from the top with a needle and thread or wrap.

4 To wrap, make a loop in the thread and position this lying on top of the tassel threads. Take the wrapping thread tightly around the tassel five or six times. Finish off by threading the end through the loop (Fig. 7).

5 Pull loop up tightly to take opposite end underneath wrap (Fig. 7). Trim the tails close to the wrapping.

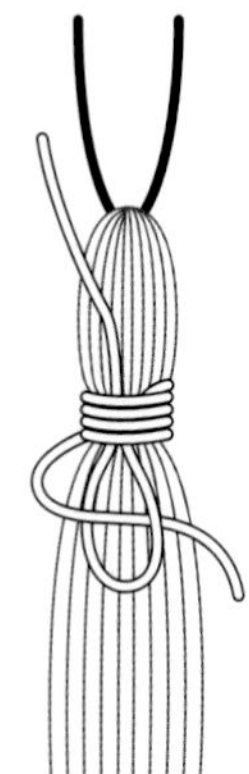

Fig. 7

6 Trim the tassel ends and if necessary, steam gently over water to 'fluff out' the fibres.

Alternative ideas and suggestions

- Change the colour of the roses.
- Use small beads for the centres of the roses instead of French knots.
- Use small beads for the centres of the forget-me-nots instead of French knots.
- Replace the thread tassels with beaded tassels.
- Dye your own fabric and threads.

KEY

Use one strand of Mulberry silk throughout or two strands of Anchor stranded cotton (floss).

Bullion Roses

A = large

B = medium

C = small

	Stitch	Number of wraps	Colour
A			
Centre	3 French knots	2	Dark yellow
Next layer	3 Bullion knots	9	Medium yellow
Outer layer	7 Bullion knots	12	Pale yellow
Outer petals (round lower edge)	4 Bullion knots	9	Pale yellow
B			
Centre	3 French knots	1	Dark yellow
Next layer	3 Bullion knots	7	Medium yellow
Outer layer	7 Bullion knots	9	Pale yellow
C			
Centre	3 French knots	1	Dark yellow
Next layer	3 Bullion knots	7	Medium yellow
Outer layer	5 Bullion knots	9	Pale yellow
Buds			
Centre	2 Bullion knots	5	Medium or pale yellow
Outer layer	1 or 2 Fly stitches		Lighter green
Leaves	Detached chain		Dark or light green
Stems	Stem stitch		Dark green
Forget-me-nots			
Centre	1 French knot	1	Pale yellow
Outer petals	5 French knots	1	Blue

Floral design

The design is 80% of the actual size. Please enlarge on the photocopier by 125%.

'Harmony' Herb Pillow Bolster

This herb pillow, filled with soothing camomile or healing lavender, looks stunning in any bedroom, the perfect setting for heirloom sewing techniques on fine cotton lawn with Swiss beading, cotton insertion and edging laces, ribbons and pintucks. The central band is left plain for you to personalize as you wish, and the simple construction means that the pillow can be easily washed and the herbs changed to match your mood. Use it as a neck support filled with calming herbs or simply enjoy the pillow as part of your bedroom decoration.

Finished size: *Approx. 35.5cm (14in) long, 18cm (7in) wide*

Materials

1.2m (1⅜yd) white cotton lawn/voile/batiste, 112cm (44in) wide

2 reels fine white sewing cotton (Mettler Cotton 60/2)

2.4m (2½yd) Swiss embroidered beading with entredeux both sides

2.3m (2⅜yd) Swiss cotton edging lace

3m (3¼yd) white satin ribbon, 6mm (¼in) wide

White cotton gimp or DMC Coton Perlé No. 8 for corded pintucks

Twin needle size 80/2 and pintucking foot

Fabric marking pencil

1m (1⅛yd) elastic, 6mm (¼in) wide

Spray starch

35.5cm (14in) bolster cushion pad, circumference 53.3cm (21in)

Small herb sachet

Instructions

1 Read and refer to the section on heirloom sewing techniques, pages 20-23. Straighten the edge of the lawn by pulling a thread before cutting. Press seams as you work.

2 Cut pieces in lawn as follows:

Frill	2 pieces 10 x 112cm (4 x 44in)
Casing end	12.7 x 112 cm (5 x 44in)
Centre piece	7.6 x 53.3cm (3 x 21in)
Lining	53.3 x 50.8cm (21 x 20in)

3 For the pintucking, mark a strip 12.7 x 112cm (5 x 44in), but do not cut off until pintucking is completed.

4 Join the shorter sides of the lining with a French seam. To form casing at each end, turn under 12mm (½in), press and turn under a further 12mm (½in). Machine stitch close to the folded edge, leaving an opening for the elastic. Pull the bolster pad through the fabric tube. Thread elastic through each casing, pull up tightly to form a circle. Knot the elastic and hide ends in the casing.

5 Attach the edging lace to one side of the frill piece. Roll and whip each end of the frill. Set the width so that the needle goes into the fabric and outside it to give a neat rolled and whipped edge. Stitch three rows of gathering on the side opposite the lace.

6 Draw a straight line 1.5cm (⅝in) from the seam edge to mark the first line of pintucking or use a machine seam guide attachment to keep you straight. Set up your twin needle and pintucking foot. If you have a grooved pintuck foot, your rows will sit in grooves to keep the machining straight and the tucks equally distanced. If not, make a simple spacer out of card the exact width of the finished tuck and mark in the lines. Stitch 5cm (2in) of pintucking down the entire length of the fabric strip, with each tuck 6mm (¼in) apart. Leave 15mm (⅝in) from the last tuck before trimming excess fabric.

7 Carefully press the pintucked band onto a towel before cutting it in half to make two bands 53.3cm (21in) long. Lightly starch the Swiss beading and cut four pieces 53.3cm (21in) long keeping the repeats equal. Attach beading to either side of each of the pintucked bands. Join the pintucked bands to either side of the middle piece of fabric.

8 Pull up the gathers on the frill to 50.8cm (20in). With right sides together, place the unattached side of the Swiss beading on top of the gathers. Position the rolled edge of the frill 12mm (½in) away from each end of the beading. Pin in position. Cut casing end piece of fabric in half to measure 53.3cm (21in) long. Place beading and frill on top of the 'casing end' fabric (wrong side of frill to right side of fabric). Tack (baste) the three thicknesses together with white cotton thread exactly where you will be straight

stitching against the side of the entredeux. Join the frill and casing end to each pintucked band.

9 Join fabric lengthwise with a French seam, to line up with the edge of the frill, avoiding catching the frill in the seam.

10 Form casing as for the lining.

11 Thread ribbon through the beading and tie bows on the top of the pillow before pulling pillow through the fabric tube.

12 Tuck herb sachets in each end of the pillow before pulling up the elastic tightly. Secure the elastic with a knot, ease and hide ends inside the casing.

Alternative ideas and suggestions

- Space the pintucks more widely and use one of the built-in patterns on your sewing machine to add interest (a backing paper will be necessary to support the pattern).
- Use a wing needle to create hemstitching effects with simple built-in patterns on the sewing machine. Combine with satin stitch lines or pintucking (Stitch 'n' Tear backing or a liquid fabric stabiliser will be needed to prevent distortion).
- Stitch the pintucks in coloured thread and combine with coloured ribbon.
- Appliqué narrow satin ribbon between the wider pintucks.
- Embroider initials in the central panel.
- Use a commercially embroidered band for the central panel.
- Stitch the pintucks in coloured thread and combine with coloured ribbon.

CHAPTER 3

NEW ARRIVALS

This chapter celebrates new arrivals and the birth of a new baby. The projects use four different embroidery techniques.

A soft shawl to welcome a baby, embroidered with surface stitchery.

A Hardanger embroidered Christening cracker edged with beads which not only holds a present but is also decorative.

A Christening gown of fine lawn with heirloom sewing and yards of beautiful lace and delicate hand embroidery.

A cot quilt, in practical blue with crisp, white Sashiko quilting which can be used as a wall hanging in later life.

'Star Attraction' Welcome Shawl With Surface Embroidery

This welcome shawl of hearts and roses embroidered in softest pink, blue, yellow and green on the lightest of woollen fabrics is designed to envelop your special baby in love. The rich surface embroidery will ensure that your precious bundle is the star attraction and that this will be a shawl for future generations to enjoy and treasure.

The shawl is double sided, with a large heart design on one corner and smaller hearts on the other three corners on the reverse. When the shawl is folded for use, the embroidery is shown to full advantage.

Finished size: *89 x 89cm (35 x 35in)*

Materials

2m (2½yd) fine white or cream wool, Viyella, or challis, 112cm (44in) wide. Extra ½m (½yd) for piping (optional)

1 skein each of Anchor stranded cotton as follows: 894 (dark pink), 73 (pale pink), 130 (dark blue), 120 (light blue), 300 (pale yellow), 214 (green)

Straw needle size 8 (for bullions)

Crewel needle size 9

Sewing thread to match fabric

Pastel-coloured tacking (basting) cotton

Small embroidery hoop

4m (4½yd) fine piping cord or pastel satin bias ribbon (optional)

Quilters Ultimate marking pencil

Tracing paper

Instructions

1 Read and refer to the section on surface embroidery techniques and stitches, pages 34-37. Cut two pieces of fabric 91.5 x 91.5cm (36 x 36in).

2 Trace the heart designs on to tracing paper.

3 Taking one piece of fabric, fold one corner in half to find the diagonal centre line XY (Fig. 1).

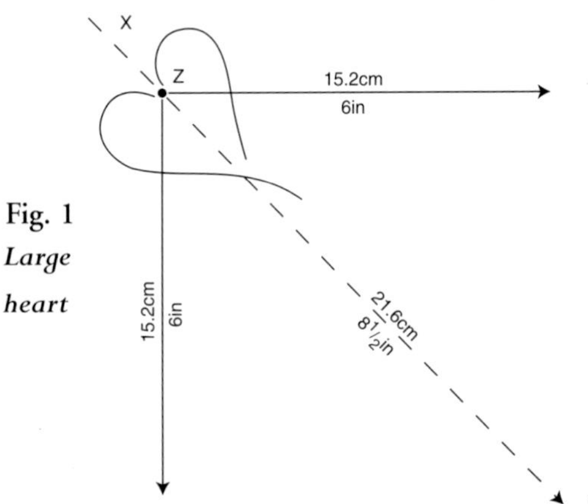

Fig. 1 ***Large heart***

Gently press the crease. Place this corner of fabric over the larger traced heart design, positioning it as shown, with point Z on the diagonal crease. Repeat on three corners of the other piece of fabric, but positioning the smaller heart nearer to the corners as shown in Fig. 2.

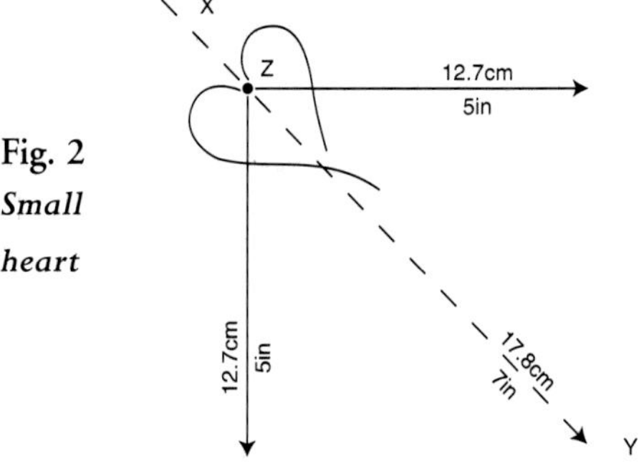

Fig. 2
Small heart

4 Using the marking pencil, gently mark circles for the bullion roses, small crosses for the daisies, dots for the forget-me-not centres, two curved lines for the buds and one short curved line for the leaves. Extra single leaves can be added if you need to fill spaces.

5 Place the marked fabric in the hoop. Referring to the key, stitch the designs in the following order. First the bullion roses, then the detached-chain daisies, small buds and forget-me-nots. Finally, fill in the spaces with small detached-chain leaves.

6 If necessary, carefully hand wash the finished embroidery using a mild soap powder. Dry face down on towelling and stretch carefully into shape. Press lightly on the back.

Making up the Shawl

1 For a piped edge, tack (baste) the piping to the right side of the piece of fabric with the large embroidered heart, 12mm (½in) from the edge of the fabric. Overlap the ends

carefully for a neat join. I prefer sharp corners but if a softer shape is preferred, gently curve the piping on the corners.

2 Position the two pieces of fabric right sides together, taking care to position the unembroidered corner of the second piece of fabric against the corner with the large embroidered heart on the first piece. Machine stitch 12mm (½in) from the edge, leaving a 10cm (4in) gap along one edge. Trim excess fabric, clip corner curves and turn inside out. Ladderstitch the opening together.

3 Alternatively, for a satin binding, place the two pieces of fabric wrong sides together, place one edge of the binding on the edge of the fabric, right sides together, and machine stitch in place. Turn shawl over and hem other edge of binding into place.

4 Press lightly, face down on a soft towel.

Alternative ideas and suggestions

- Embroider an initial in the centre of the heart.
- Embellish the piping with stitching such as whipped chain or knotted coral stitch.
- Join the two pieces of fabric without piping and edge with an edging stitch such as Antwerp edging.
- Attach a frill instead of piping.

KEY

Use two strands of Anchor stranded thread (floss) throughout.

Bullion Roses

A = large

B = medium

C = small

	Stitch	Number of wraps	Colour
A			
Centre	3 French knots	1	Dark pink 894
Inner layer	3 Bullion knots	7	Dark pink 894
Outer layer	7 Bullion knots	9	Pale pink 73
B			
Centre	3 French knots	1	Dark pink 894
Inner layer	3 Bullion knots	7	Dark pink 894
Outer layer	5 Bullion knots	9	Pale pink 73
C			
Centre	3 French knots	1	Dark pink 894
Outer layer	3 Bullion knots	9	Pale pink 73
Daisies			
Centre	1 or 3 French knots	1	Yellow 300
Petals	6 Detached chain stitches		Yellow 300
Buds			
Centre	2 Bullion knots	5	Dark pink 894
Outer layer	1 Fly stitch		Green 214
Stems	Stem stitch		Green 214
Leaves	Detached chain stitch		Green 214
Forget-me-nots			
Centre	1 French knot	1	Yellow 300
Petals	5 French knots	1	Dark blue 130

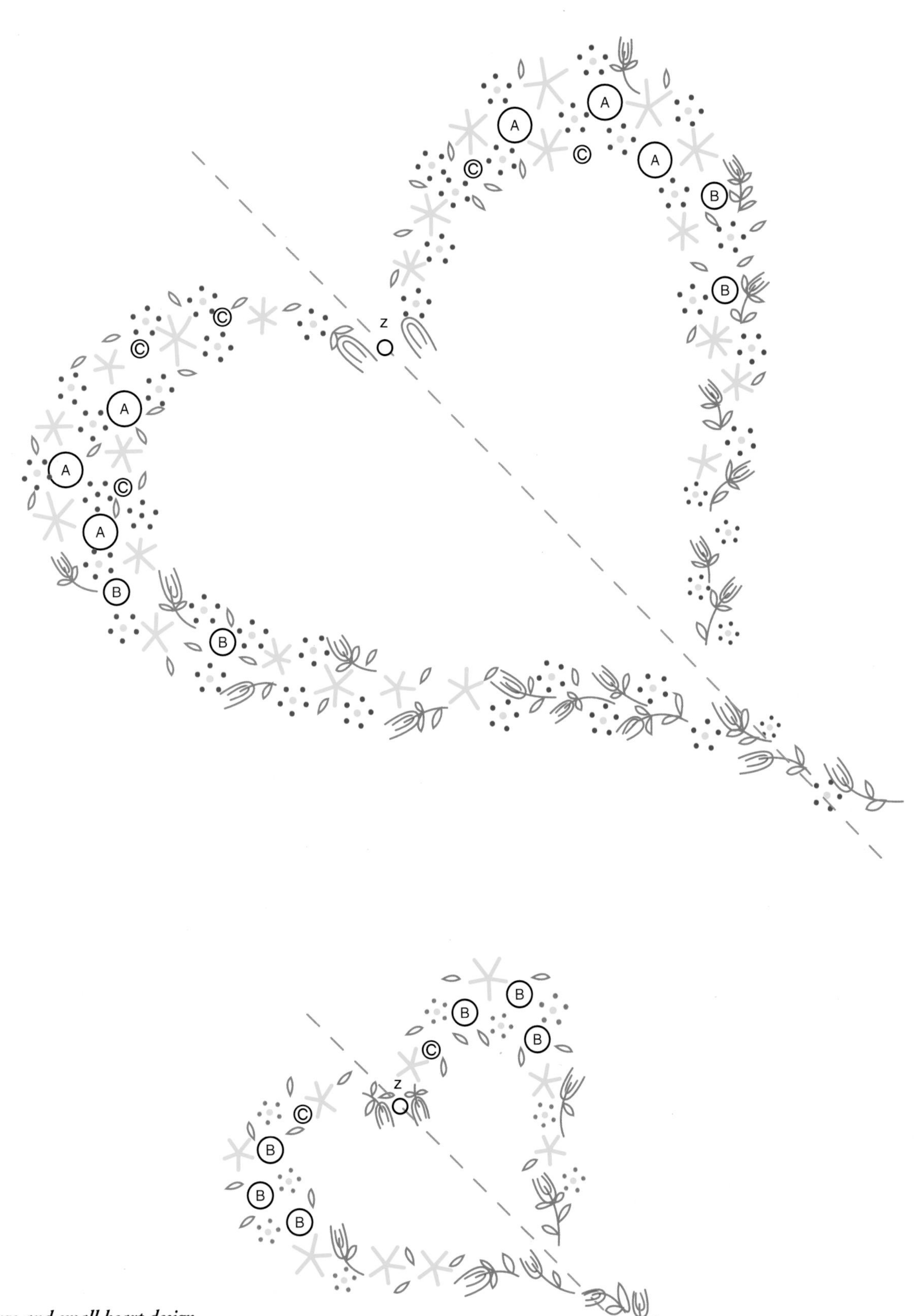

Large and small heart design
Actual size.

'Serendipity' Hardanger Christening Cracker

Deliver your Christening present in this unique and enduring fabric cracker and you are sure to make an impression. The pastel-coloured lining highlights the Hardanger embroidery design, which is combined with satin ribbon and pearl beads. Simply undo the ribbons to slip in the present. After the Christening, it could be used for decoration – perhaps filled with pot pourri.

Finished size: *32cm (12⅝in),*
circumference: *16cm (6¼in)*

Materials

22 x 38cm (8¾ x 15in) white evenweave linen, 26 threads to the inch

DMC Coton Perlé white No. 8 and No.12 (1 reel of each)

Small pearl beads (optional)

80cm (32in) white satin ribbon, 1.5mm (⅝in) wide

1m (1¼yd) cord or ribbon for tying cracker

Pale-coloured tacking (basting) thread

Tapestry needle size 24

Fine, sharp-pointed scissors

Beading needle and polyester thread for beads

22 x 38cm (8¾ x 15in) coloured fabric for lining

11.5cm (4½in) toilet roll, diameter 4.5cm (1¾in)

Spray mount or fabric glue

Double-sided tape

11.5 x 16cm (4½ x 6¼in) white felt to cover toilet roll

11.5 x 14 cm (4½ x 5½in) wrapping paper or felt for lining inside of toilet roll (optional)

Instructions

1 Read and refer to the section on Hardanger techniques and stitches, pages 24-33. Prepare the linen as described.

2 To line the toilet roll, place double-sided tape on the two shorter sides of the paper or felt. Peel off backing, form the lining carefully into a roll and push down into the centre of the toilet roll. Press one side into position and then overlap the other. Cover the outside of the toilet roll with felt, sticking the felt in place with glue. Trim so that the edges meet but do not overlap.

3 Follow the chart and key to establish the central pattern.

Row 1 Starting at A, stitch a row of Kloster blocks; work from the centre on each side.

Row 2 Stitch the straight edging line of Kloster blocks, ensuring the blocks are in line with the previous row.

Row 3 Work the half-star motif; start at B.

Rows 4 & 5 Turn the work upside down to stitch the diagonal eyelets beginning at C, followed by the half square eyelet in the centre of the star.

Row 6 Start reversed diagonal faggoting at a point.

Rows 7 & 8 For the row of hem stitches forming the casing, count 14 threads (towards the outer edge) from the Kloster block edging worked in Row 2. Cut 8 horizontal threads 3cm (1⅛in) from each side edge and remove the loose centre threads. Carefully unravel the remaining ends, fold back into the seam and secure with back stitches (see page 32). Work the two rows of hem stitch opposite each other, turning the work to complete the second row.

Row 9 Count 72 threads from the top line of hem stitching (Row 8) and stitch the twisted lattice band.

Rows 10, 11 & 12 Repeat the star motif, diagonal and half eyelets as before.

Row 13 Now you are ready to cut the threads from the centre of the design. In this case, do not cut the horizontal threads against the sides of the design, but leave enough horizontal thread to turn back and secure as with hem stitching (see page 32).

Row 14 Proceed with the needleweaving, stitching the dove's eye filling as you go. Work in steps across the design from top right to bottom left.

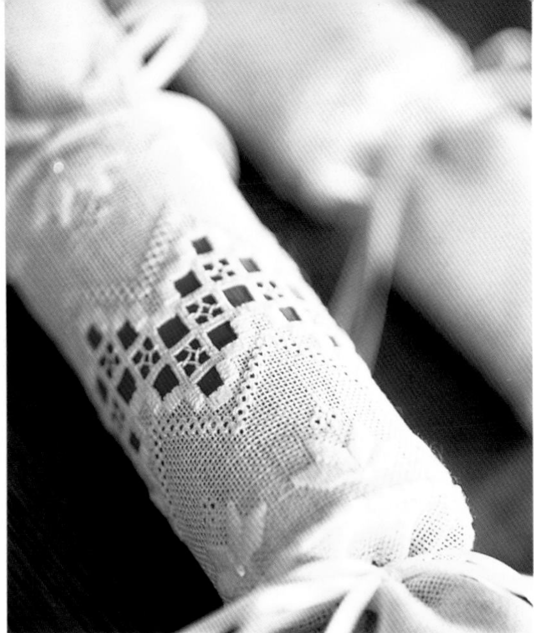

Row 15 Sew pearls (if desired) in the centres of the star motifs. The pearl edging is completed once the cracker is made up.

Row 16 Thread the white satin ribbon through the Kloster blocks and twisted lattice band, keeping it flat.

4 If necessary, wash carefully and press.

Making up the Cracker

1 Place the coloured lining fabric and embroidery right sides together. Tack (baste) together two threads in from the edge of the design (in the middle of the last Kloster block) starting level with Row 2 of the design to the end of the cracker. Tack (baste) along the top of the cracker four threads above the twisted lattice band, and continue

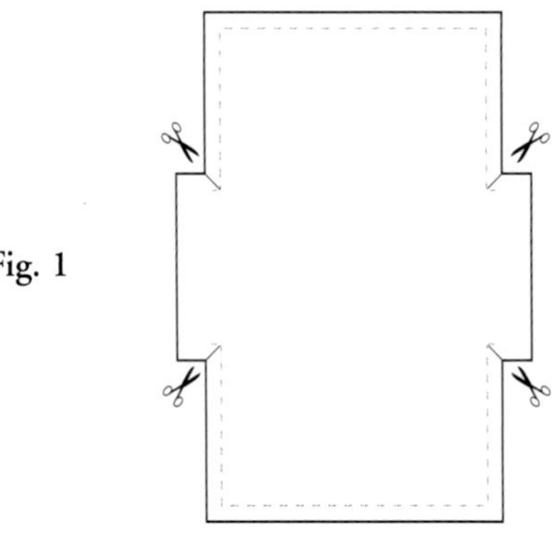

Fig. 1

down the other side as before (Fig. 1). Repeat at the other end, leaving the middle open.

2 Machine stitch together and trim (Fig. 1). Turn inside out so that the middle part sticks out like wings. Neaten the raw edges.

3 To form the casing, machine stitch the two fabrics together on both sides of the hem stitching. Thread ribbon or cord through the casing, leaving the ends loose.

4 Sew on pearl beads if wished on the edge of the cracker above the twisted lattice band.

5 Wrap the embroidery round the covered toilet roll, allowing one edge of the unstitched seam to lie flat against the roll. Fix into position with pins. Fold the other unstitched edge under and position over the flat seam so that the design is continuous and the edges are just touching. Ladderstitch the seam edges together.

6 Put in the present before pulling up the cord or ribbons.

Alternative ideas and suggestions

- Use French knots instead of pearls on the edge of the cracker.
- Work the twisted lattice band in a colour to match the lining.
- Thread contrasting ribbon through the twisted lattice band and Kloster blocks.
- Use pale pink or blue linen instead of white, or change the lining colour.
- Choose a narrow contrasting ribbon/ribbons for the ties.
- Change the filling stitch.
- Add tassels or beads to the end of the ribbon ties.

KEY

Each grid line represents one thread of fabric. The chart shows half of the design; repeat for the other half.

Rows 1 & 2
Kloster blocks
DMC Coton Perlé No. 8

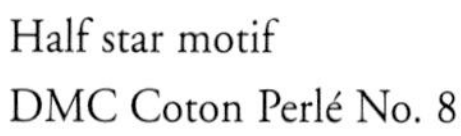

Rows 3 & 10
Half star motif
DMC Coton Perlé No. 8

Rows 4 & 11
Diagonal eyelets
DMC Coton Perlé No. 12

Rows 5 & 12
Half square eyelet
DMC Coton Perlé No. 12

Row 6
Reversed diagonal faggoting
DMC Coton Perlé No. 12

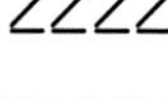

Rows 7 & 8
Hem stitching
DMC Coton Perlé No. 12

Row 9
Twisted lattice band
DMC Coton Perlé No. 8

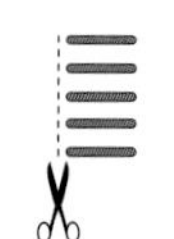

Row 13
Cut threads

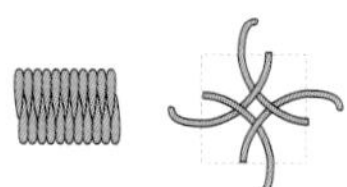

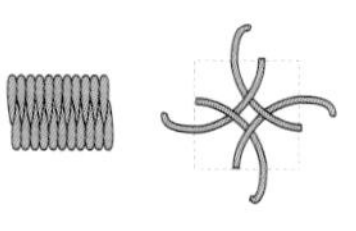

Row 14
Needleweaving and dove's eyes
DMC Coton Perlé No. 12

● Centrepoint

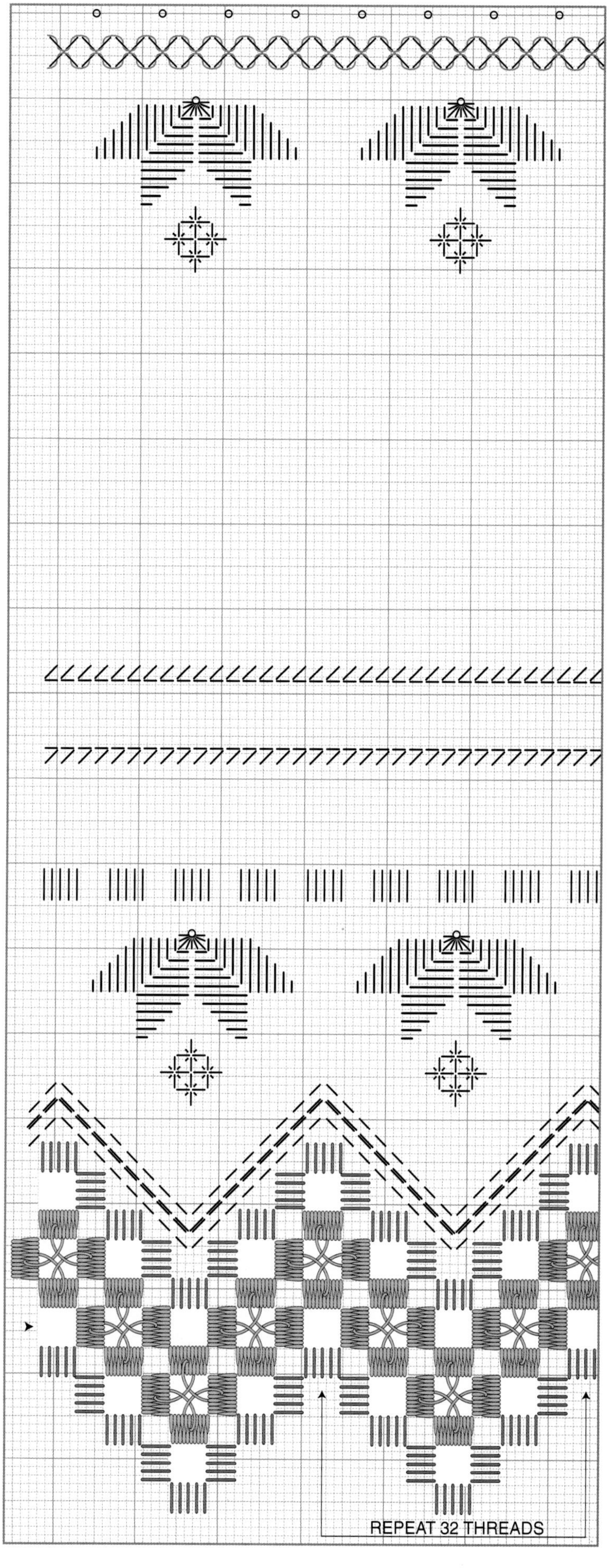

REPEAT 32 THREADS

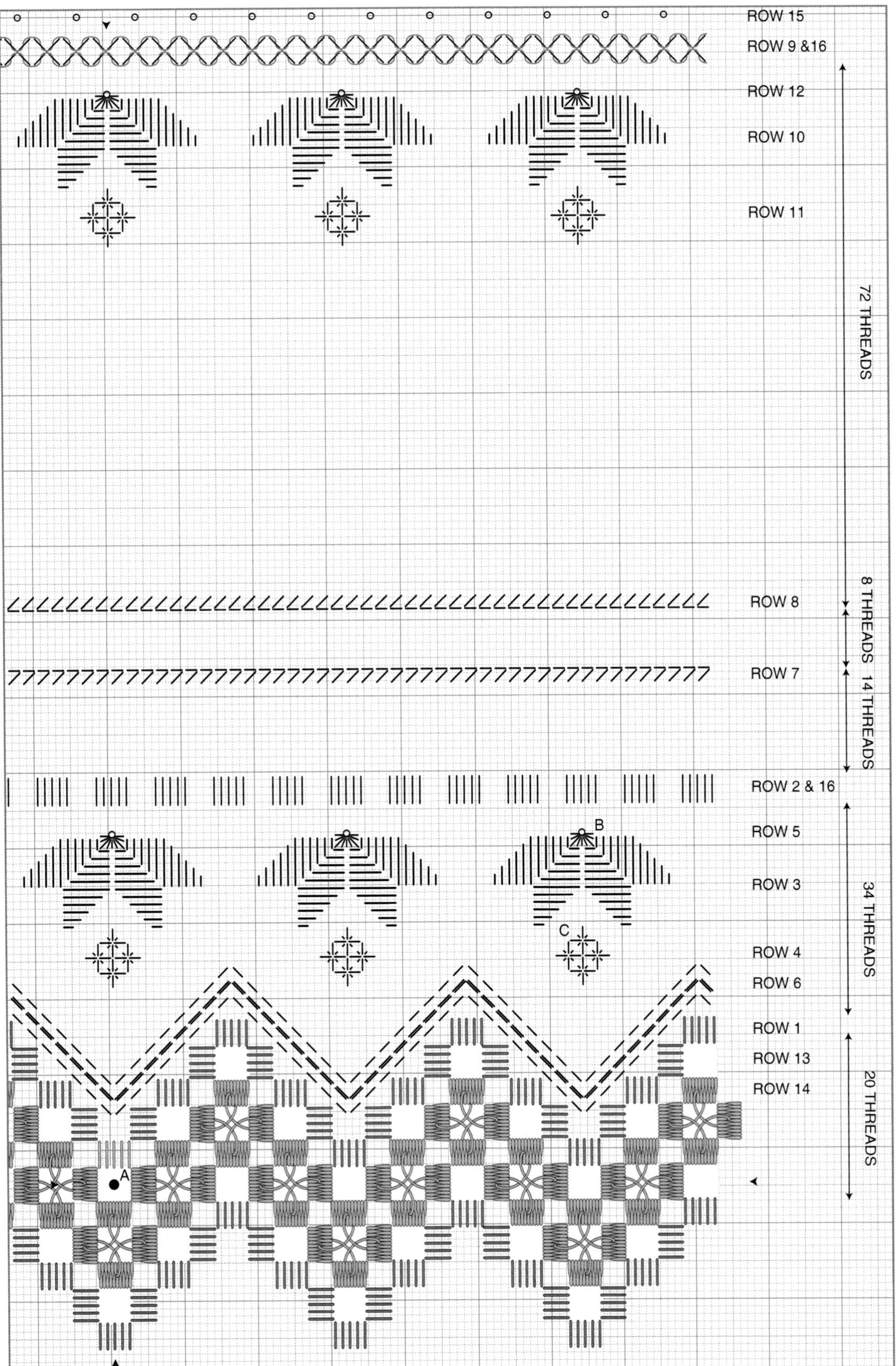
ROW 15
ROW 9 &16
ROW 12
ROW 10
ROW 11
72 THREADS
ROW 8
8 THREADS
ROW 7
14 THREADS
ROW 2 & 16
B
ROW 5
ROW 3
34 THREADS
C
ROW 4
ROW 6
ROW 1
ROW 13
ROW 14
20 THREADS
A

'Innocence' Christening Gown With Surface Embroidery

Daisies, for innocence, decorate this simple but enchanting Christening gown creating a dress to be cherished. The delicate hand embroidery on fine cotton lawn with lace insertions make it an inheritance for the future. Traditionally shaped, the dress is easy to construct – and if you love to machine, look again at all those exciting built-in patterns on your machine which could easily replace the hand embroidery.

Finished length from shoulder: *104cm (41in)*

Materials

2.2m (2⅜yd) white cotton lawn, voile, or batiste, 112cm (44in) wide

1.2m (1⅜yd) French insertion lace, 1cm (⅜in) wide

4.5m (4⅞yd) French insertion lace, 1.5cm (⅝in) wide

3.2m (3½yd) entredeux

1.2m (1⅜yd) Swiss embroidered beading with entredeux both sides

0.5m (20in) narrow French edging lace

0.7m (¾yd) medium French edging lace, 1.5-2cm (⅝-¾in) wide

4m (4⅜yd) deep French edging lace, 5cm (2in) wide

3.25m (3¾yd) white satin ribbon, 6mm (¼in) wide

Fine white sewing thread

Fine white silk embroidery thread: Mulberry Silk No. W800, Madeira Silk or stranded cotton (floss)

Sharps needle size 10

2 small pearl buttons

Small pearl beads

Small embroidery hoop

Pastel-coloured tacking (basting) cotton

Quilters Ultimate marking pencil

Spray starch

Tracing paper

For the petticoat, you will need the same requirements again.

Instructions

1 Read and refer to the sections on heirloom sewing techniques and surface embroidery, pages 20-23 and 34-37. Allow 1cm (⅜in) seam allowances throughout. Press the pieces carefully after each stage.

Bodice

1 Trace the three pattern pieces, incorporating all guide lines and markings (pages 83-85).

2 Cut a square of fabric 18 x 36cm (7 x 14⅛in) and lay bodice front pattern over the fabric. Tack (baste) round the outline using pastel thread.

3 Press and lightly starch the narrow insertion lace and pin onto fabric square following the pattern guide lines. Tack (baste) slightly away from the edge then machine stitch along the edges of the lace using a fine zigzag.

4 Lay the bodice front over the tracing. Lightly trace the embroidery design between the lace insertions. Note: the fabric piece will have shrunk slightly after the lace insertions have been stitched, so centre the embroidery design between each lace insertion.

5 Work the embroidery using a single strand. The daisy petals are stitched in detached chain with one straight satin stitch down the middle. The stems are stitched in stem stitch with detached chain for the leaves. Sew on the beads at the centres of the flowers (see key on page 82). Press right side down into a towel.

6 Place the bodice pattern on the embroidered bodice again, check the outline and cut out the bodice. Stay stitch the neckline.

7 Carefully trim away the fabric from behind the lace insertions, starting by cutting centrally down the length, then trimming to 2mm (under ⅛in) at each side (Fig. 1).

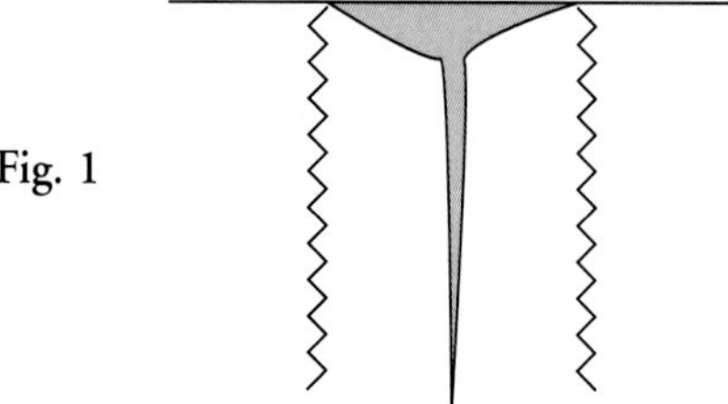

Fig. 1

Making up the bodice

1 Cut out the bodice back sections. Fold under both centre-back edges 12mm (½in), press, then fold under a further 12mm (½in). Press and stitch close to the edge. Stay stitch the neckline.

2 Stitch together the bodice front and back at the shoulders using French seams.

3 Machine stitch entredeux to the armhole edges, but clipping one side of the entredeux fabric to allow for the curve.

4 Stitch entredeux to the neck edge as for the armhole. Trim the outer edge of the entredeux. Gather narrow French edging lace and stitch it to the entredeux.

5 Make two buttonholes on left-hand bodice back. Sew buttons on the other side to match.

Sleeves

1 Cut out the sleeves. Tailor tack the large black dot and tack (baste) along the centre fold line.

2 Trace the embroidery motif from the sleeve pattern onto the sleeve. Embroider the design as before and press.

3 For the cuffs, make three rows of gathering on the lower edge of the sleeves to 18cm (7⅛in), stitching the first line of gathering 1cm (⅜in) from the edge and a further line either side of this. Distribute the gathers evenly. Place Swiss embroidered beading on the sleeves, with the edge of the beading's entredeux on the middle gathered line and a ribbon opening in the centre of the sleeve. Stitch in position. Remove the visible line of gathering. Gather medium French edging lace and attach it to the entredeux on the other edge of the Swiss embroidered beading.

4 Make two lines of gathers on the upper edges of the sleeves, between the dots. Ease to fit the armholes, distributing the gathers evenly. Attach the sleeves to the entredeux around the armholes.

5 Join underarms and bodice sides with French seams.

6 At the lower edge of bodice, attach the entredeux of more Swiss embroidered beading, folding under 6mm (¼in) at the back seam.

Skirt

1 Cut out two main panels 80cm (31½in) x width of fabric. Fold in half and tack (baste) along the centre line back and front. Join one side in a French seam.

2 Starch and press the wider French insertion lace and join to lower edge of skirt.

3 Cut out two further strips of fabric 5.5cm (2¼in) x width of fabric, joining one side in a French seam. Attach this flat strip to the lace insertion at the lower edge of the skirt. Pin from the French seam out, to allow for any slight stretching of the insertion lace. Attach a further piece of the wider French insertion lace to the lower edge. Trim the side edges of the skirt section if necessary.

4 Join the remaining skirt side seam with a French seam.

5 Trim the edge from one side of a piece of entredeux and butt it (right sides up) to the lace insertion at the lower edge of the skirt, overlapping slightly at the join.

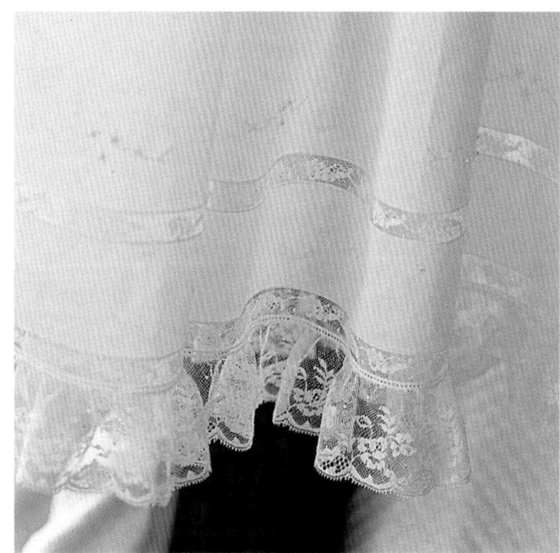

6 Lightly trace the two rows of embroidery design on to the skirt as described for the bodice, alternating the motifs (see above). Measure 3cm (1⅛in) up from the top layer of insertion lace to the centre of the top daisy on the motif. Place the first motif on the centre front of the skirt, with each motif 15cm (6in) apart (from centre to centre of

top daisy). I suggest marking the placement of the motifs with pins around the skirt prior to tracing to ensure the motifs are equally distributed. Alter the distance between motifs if necessary. Alternate a reversed motif if preferred. The lower motifs fall between the motifs of the top row. Work the embroidery on the skirt as described for the sleeves.

7 Trim the lower edge of the entredeux at the lower edge of the skirt. Gather deep French edging lace and butt it (right sides up) to this entredeux, overlapping at side join. Stitch down the overlapped lace using a small zigzag stitch, and trim away excess.

8 Make a continuous placket for the centre back as shown in Fig. 2. To make the placket, cut a strip of lawn 4 x 16.5cm (1½ x 6½in). Make a vertical 7.5cm (3in), cut from the top edge, down the centre back. Stay stitch the point before opening the slit into a straight line. Place the right side of the strip to the right side of the fabric and machine down one side 3mm (⅛in) to the point and up the other side 3mm (⅛in). Turn under the raw edge, place the fold on the previous stitching line and stitch the edge. Fold under the left-hand side of the placket and position on top of the right hand side. Secure placket into place (at the point) with a few small stitches.

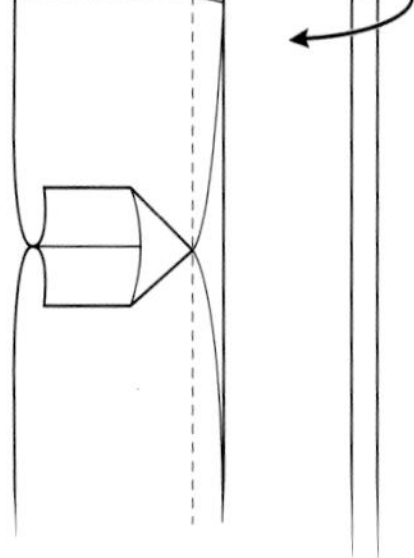

Fig. 2

9 Make three gathering lines at the top of the skirt, and pull up to gather. Stitch gathered edge of skirt to the lower edge of the beading on the bodice, matching centre fronts. Finish raw edges of the seam with zigzag stitch or a rolled hem. Press. On the right side, using a fine thread, zigzag over this seam into the entredeux of the beading to keep it lying flat.

10 Thread ribbon through the beading on the bodice and sleeves.

Petticoat

1 Make the gown again, omitting the sleeves and embroidery. Trim 6mm (¼in) off the neck and sleeve edges to make the petticoat slightly smaller than the gown.

2 Stitch entredeux and lace round the neck and armholes, or neaten with a small hem or decorative edging stitch.

Alternative ideas and suggestions

- Use built-in patterns on the sewing machine.
- Use shaded and metallic threads and beads.
- Change the colour of the ribbon.

KEY

Use a single strand throughout.

Daisy

5 detached chain with 1 straight satin stitch down the middle. Pearl bead for daisy centre.

Stem

Stem stitch with detached chain for leaves.

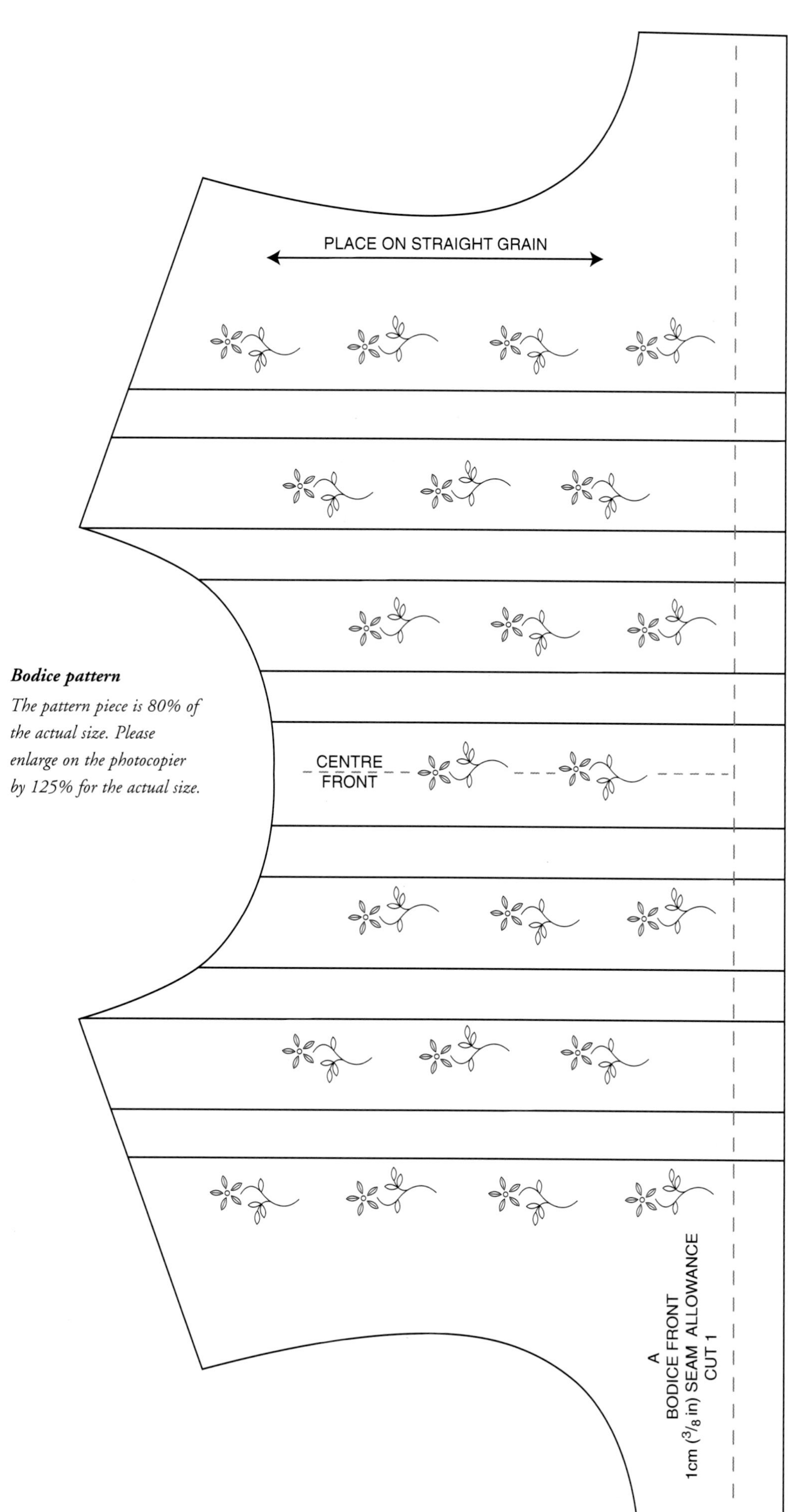

Bodice pattern

The pattern piece is 80% of the actual size. Please enlarge on the photocopier by 125% for the actual size.

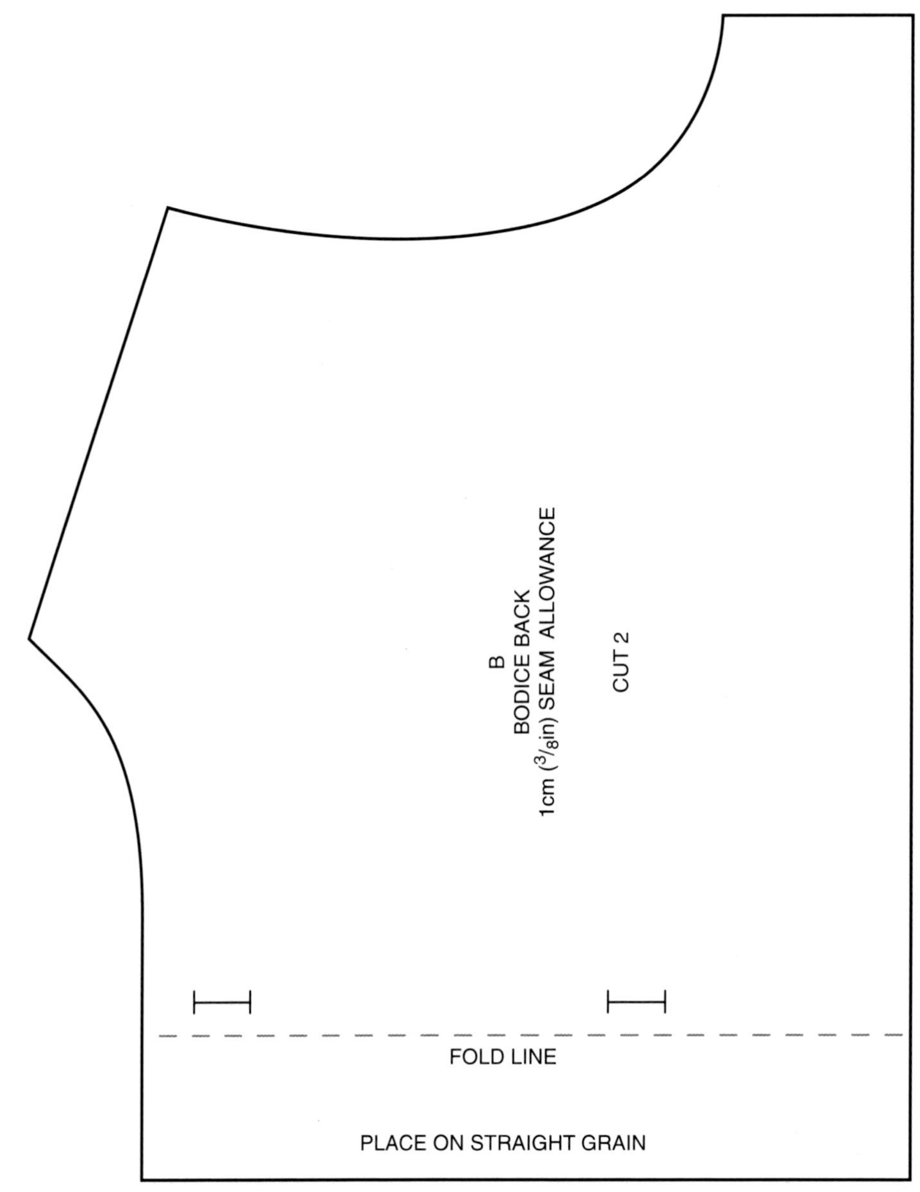

Bodice back pattern

The pattern piece is 80% of the actual size. Please enlarge on the photocopier by 125% for the actual size.

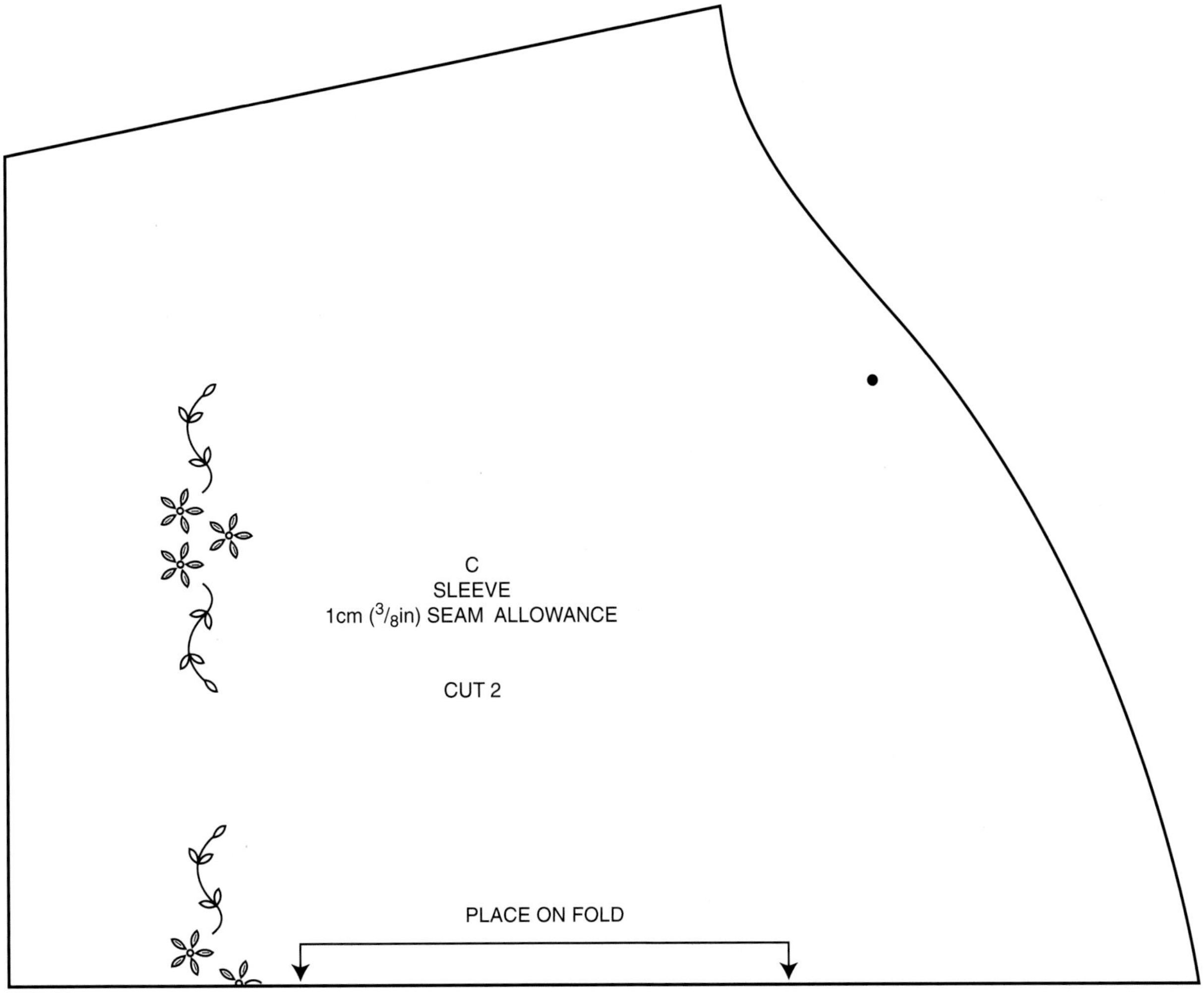

C
SLEEVE
1cm ($^{3}/_{8}$in) SEAM ALLOWANCE

CUT 2

PLACE ON FOLD

Sleeves pattern

The pattern piece is 80% of the actual size. Please enlarge on the photocopier by 125% for the actual size.

Sleeve and skirt motif

Actual size. Stitches as for bodice (see key).

'Hugo' SASHIKO COT QUILT

Japanese Sashiko quilting developed in rural Japan from stitching layers of fabric together to repair cotton clothing and to provide warmth. Items were quilted with simple straight lines of running stitches, using a heavy white thread on indigo-dyed cotton fabric. Patterns evolved and developed to become an important decorative part of the technique. They were often inspired by the surrounding countryside and recurring images are flowers, animals, waves and designs based on the hexagon or circle.

In this quilt, I have adapted traditional overlapping circles into a motif and divided the design into simple squares by lines of straight stitching. It has a central panel to enclose the baby's name, although you may prefer to use initials or a date, perhaps in a different style of lettering, or using fabric appliqué.

Finished size: *approx. 71 x 100cm (28 x 39in)*

Materials

76 x 107cm (30 x 42in) indigo-coloured or indigo-dyed 100% cotton fabric

2 x 10.2 x 76.2cm (4 x 30in) for binding as above

2 x 10.2 x 114.3cm (4 x 45in) for binding as above

81 x 112cm (32 x 44in) backing fabric

79 x 109.5cm (31 x 43in) Polyfelt needled wadding (batting)

DMC Coton Perlé white No. 8 or Sashiko cotton thread (2 reels)

Embroidery needles suitable for the thread or Clover Sashiko needles

Hera tracing tool (or used biro or bodkin)

White water-soluble marking pencil

White dressmaker's carbon paper

Masking tape

Tacking (basting) thread

Thimble

Scissors

Plastic quilter's ruler

Tracing paper

Instructions

1 Pre-wash the thread and fabric. Press the fabric. Trace the design on page 88.

2 Find and tack (baste) along the lengthwise centre line of the indigo fabric. Carefully stretch the fabric on to a smooth hard work surface, and secure with masking tape, ensuring that the grain is straight.

3 The design is based on ten squares of 20.3cm (8in) with a central rectangle of 20.3 x 40.6cm (8 x 16in). On the fabric,

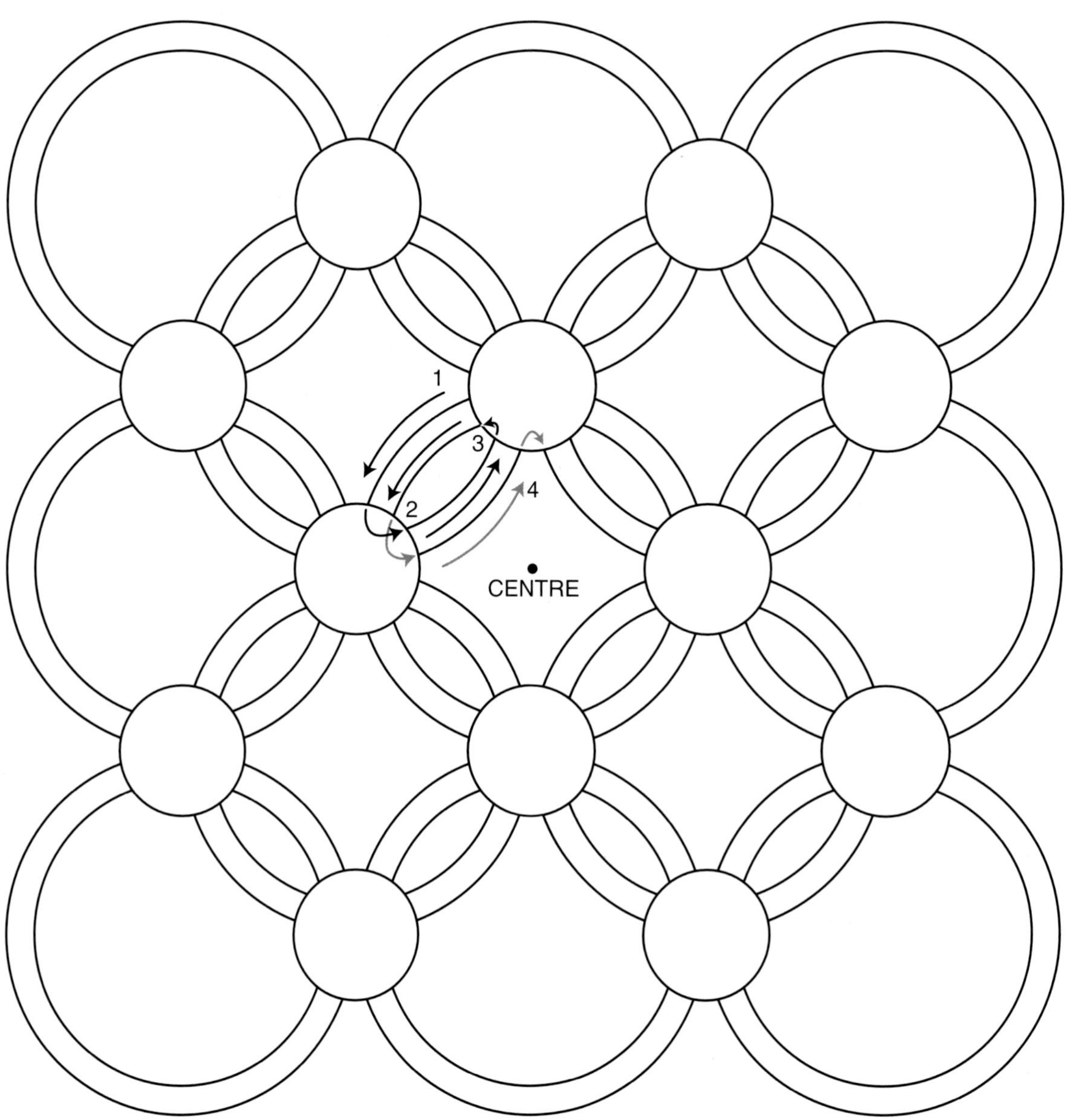

Overlapping circle motif

Fig. 1

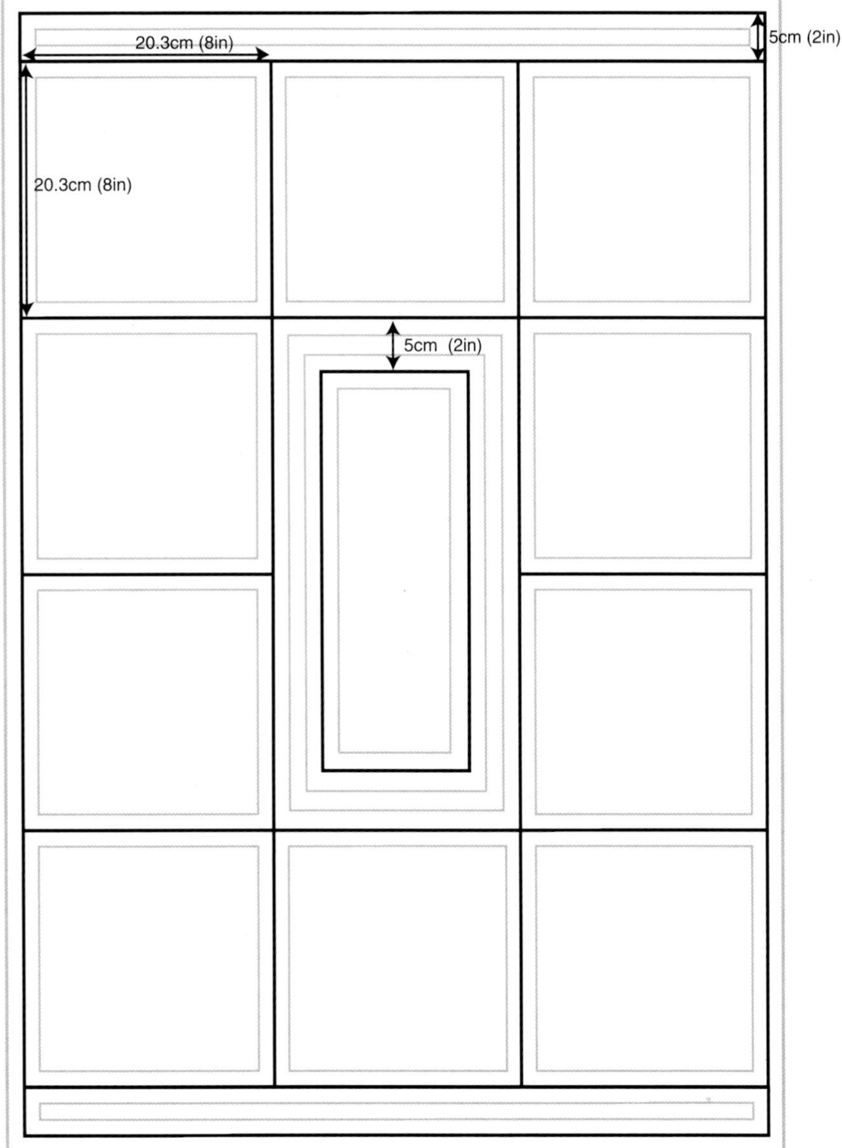

Foundation grid

draw the foundation grid as shown in Fig. 1 using your marking pencil and ruler to ensure lines are completely straight. Try not to move the fabric as you draw. Draw the inner border lines 3mm (⅛in) apart.

4 Position the traced design on top of the carbon paper in the centre of a square and secure with masking tape.

5 Using your tracing/marking tool, transfer the design onto the fabric. Repeat in the other squares. Mark your own chosen central design in the same manner.

6 Make a sandwich of the indigo fabric, wadding (batting) and backing, pinning at intervals, starting from the middle and working outwards. Tack (baste) in lines, both vertically and horizontally approximately 5cm (2in) apart.

7 Working from the middle of the quilt, stitch the foundation lines, then the inner borders. Knot the thread. From the front take the needle through the fabric, coming to the surface about 25mm (1in) away from your starting point. Pull the thread and knot carefully through the fabric so that the knot is lost in the wadding. Take a small securing back stitch before proceeding. Work four or five running stitches to the inch (two to the centimetre). Work evenly, not too tightly, with a longer length of stitch on the surface than underneath. To finish a thread, make a small knot on the surface and pull it back into the wadding. When moving from one part of the design to another, slide the needle through the sandwich so the thread will not show. Aim to make your stitches meet in a space at junctions and not cross over each other.

8 Complete the central rectangle and stitch the circle motifs, in the direction shown on page 88.

Cushion with repeat motif creating an all over design

Making up the Quilt

1 Trim the quilt to 5cm (2in) round the finished design.

2 Fold the indigo border strips in half lengthways and press the centre line (Fig. 2). Fold and press the edges into the centre fold (Fig. 3).

Fig. 2

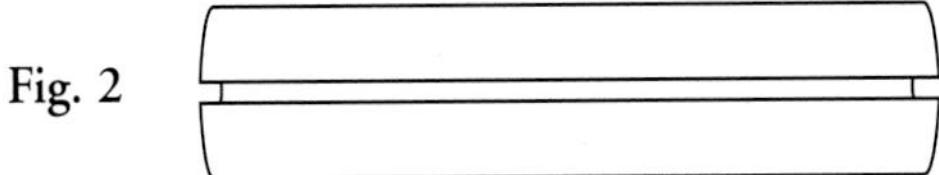

Fig. 3

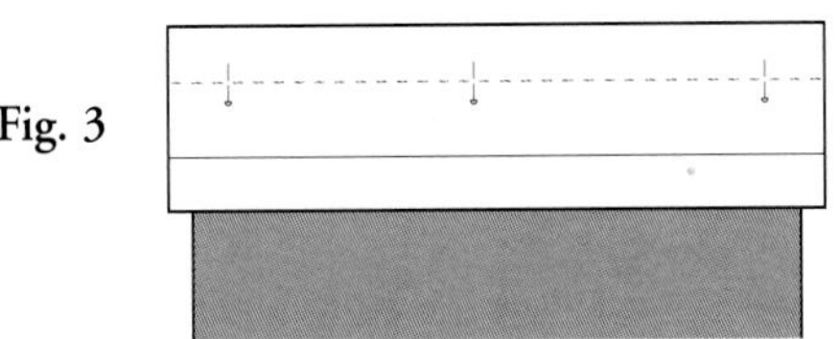

3 Open out and place one shorter piece of binding against one shorter edge of the quilt, right sides together. Machine stitch along the outer fold line. Trim the ends.

4 Fold binding over to the back so that the centre crease lies along the edge of the quilt. Tack (baste) the reverse of the binding in place, on the machine stitched line (Fig. 4).

Fig. 4

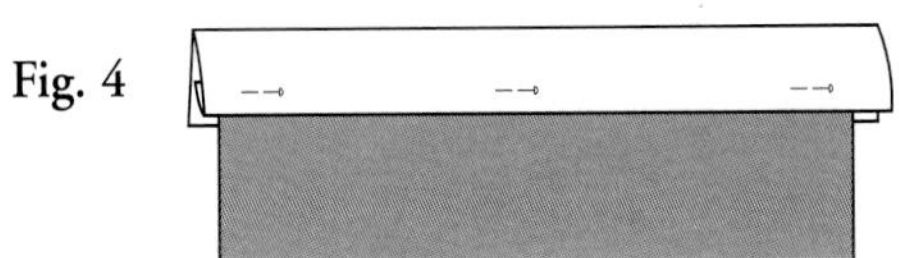

5 Repeat with the opposite border, then the other two sides. Trim and tuck in the corners to form neat right-angles. Hemstitch the binding round all sides on the reverse, into the machine stitching line.

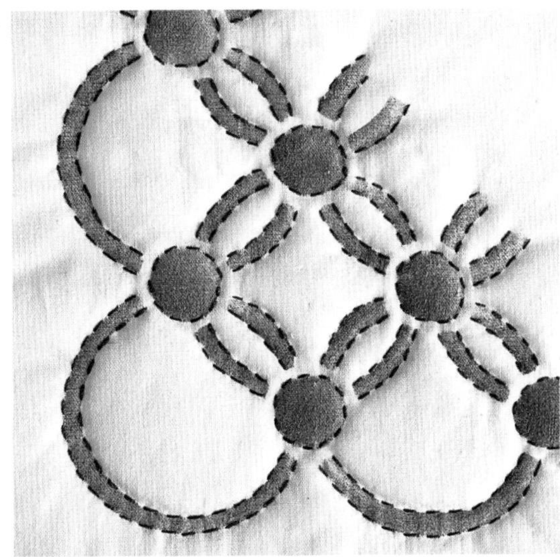

Here the design has been stencilled on white fabric

Alternative ideas and suggestions

- Extend the motif to make a larger panel for a cushion to match, missing out the centre circles to insert an initial (see photograph, left).
- Machine stitch ribbon to form the foundation grid.
- Develop the design into a stencil, fabric paint to introduce another colour and accentuate the circles (see photograph, above).
- Make it a 'lucky' quilt depicting (in the centre panel) the special Chinese characters for longevity, prosperity or good luck.
- Interpret the lettering with bias strips or use one of the built in patterns on your machine.
- Use contrasting white binding for the edges.
- Reverse the colouring, working blue stitching on white fabric.

CHAPTER 4

SPECIAL OCCASIONS

Special occasions can be anything that you want to celebrate and all the projects in this chapter could be used for any occasion. The embroidery techniques used are canvas work and Hardanger and the projects include:

A traditional sampler worked in Hardanger embroidery to make a framed panel.

A heart-shaped cushion with an all over Hardanger design brings a touch of romance.

A canvas work pin cushion with a knot garden design in pinks and greens.

A canvas work picture frame inspired by a perennially popular flower – the forget-me-not.

'Jubilee'
DRAWN THREAD SAMPLER

This classic drawn thread sampler will commemorate any occasion and give years of pleasure. It is worked on linen using matching coton perlé thread for subtlety, but with satin ribbon and glistening metallic beads to add just a little brilliance. The stitching develops from the simple to the more complicated, using all the Hardanger stitches found in this book and making this an ideal project for the newcomer to Hardanger embroidery. Change the colours to suit the celebration: blue and silver for a silver wedding, yellow and gold for a golden wedding, and black and white for a graduation.

Finished size: *16 x 31cm (6¼ x 12¼in)*

Materials

33 x 51cm (13 x 20in) cream evenweave linen, 26 threads to the inch

DMC Coton Perlé No. 8 and No. 12, colour 712 (1 reel of each)

Small metallic beads (optional)

2m (2½yd) cream satin ribbon, 1.5mm wide

Pale-coloured tacking (basting) thread

Tapestry needle size 24

Fine, sharp pointed scissors

Beading needle and thread for attaching beads

Instructions

1 Refer to the section on Hardanger techniques on pages 24-33. Prepare your linen as described.

2 Start the first row of embroidery 15.2cm (6in) up from the centre point and 7.6cm (3in) to the left of the centre point. Stitch the bands following the chart and key. Work to the centrepoint and repeat for the other half of the design. Make a point of checking that the Kloster blocks are exactly lined up, that you start on the correct thread at the beginning of each line, and that the eyelet holes are as uniform as possible.

3 Thread the satin ribbon through the casing formed by the hem stitching. Add the beads using running stitch and a back stitch after every third bead.

4 If necessary, wash carefully and dry, keeping the lines as straight as possible. Lace the embroidery on to acid-free board (see page 47) before taking it to a professional framer.

Alternative ideas and suggestions

- Put a colour behind the embroidery.
- Turn the sampler into an inset panel for a cushion.
- Make the sampler into a jewellery roll.

KEY

Each grid line represents one thread of fabric.

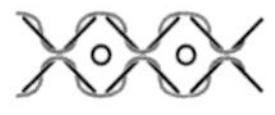

Bands 1, 5, 9
Twisted lattice band (bead in centre optional)
DMC Coton Perlé No. 8

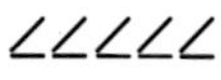

Bands 2, 4, 6, 8, 10, 12 & 14
2 rows hem stitch (4 threads apart)
DMC Coton Perlé No. 12

Bands 3, 7 & 11
Kloster blocks
DMC Coton Perlé No. 8

Bands 3, 7 & 11
Reversed diagonal faggoting
DMC Coton Perlé No. 12

Bands 3, 5, 7 & 10
Eyelets
DMC Coton Perlé No. 12

Band 5
Half star motif
DMC Coton Perlé No. 8

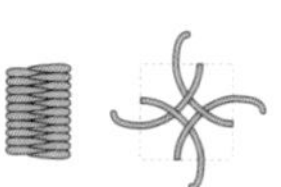

Band 7 & 11
Needleweaving with dove's eye filling
DMC Coton Perlé No. 12

Band 7
Needleweaving with French knot
DMC Coton Perlé No. 12

Band 7 and 11
Half diamond satin stitches
DMC Coton Perlé No. 8

Band 10
Linked half star motifs
DMC Coton Perlé No. 8

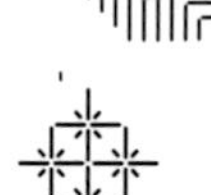

Band 10
Diagonal eyelets
DMC Coton Perlé No. 12

Band 13
2 rows of twisted lattice band (with beads in the centre line)
DMC Coton Perlé No. 8

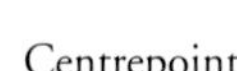

Centrepoint

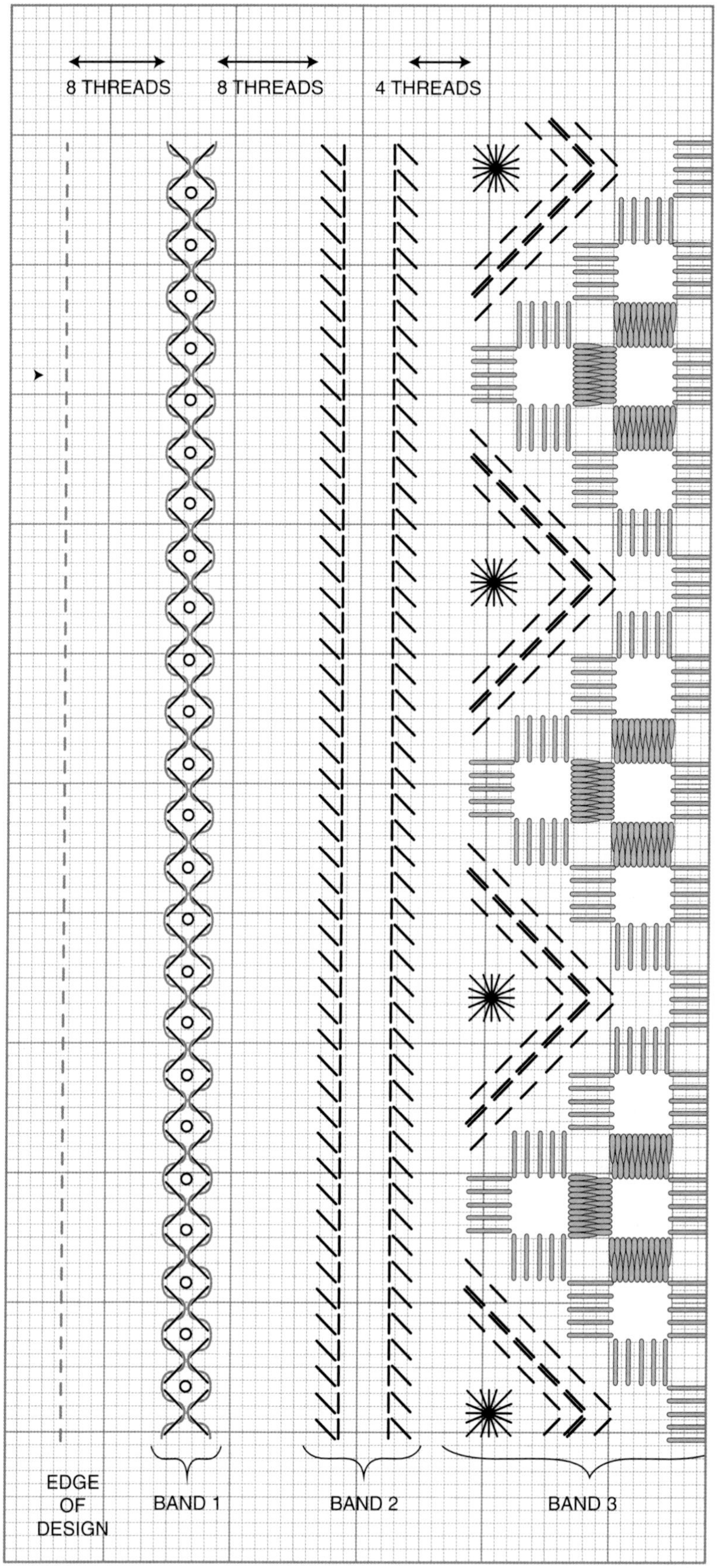

8 THREADS
8 THREADS
4 THREADS
EDGE OF DESIGN
BAND 1
BAND 2
BAND 3

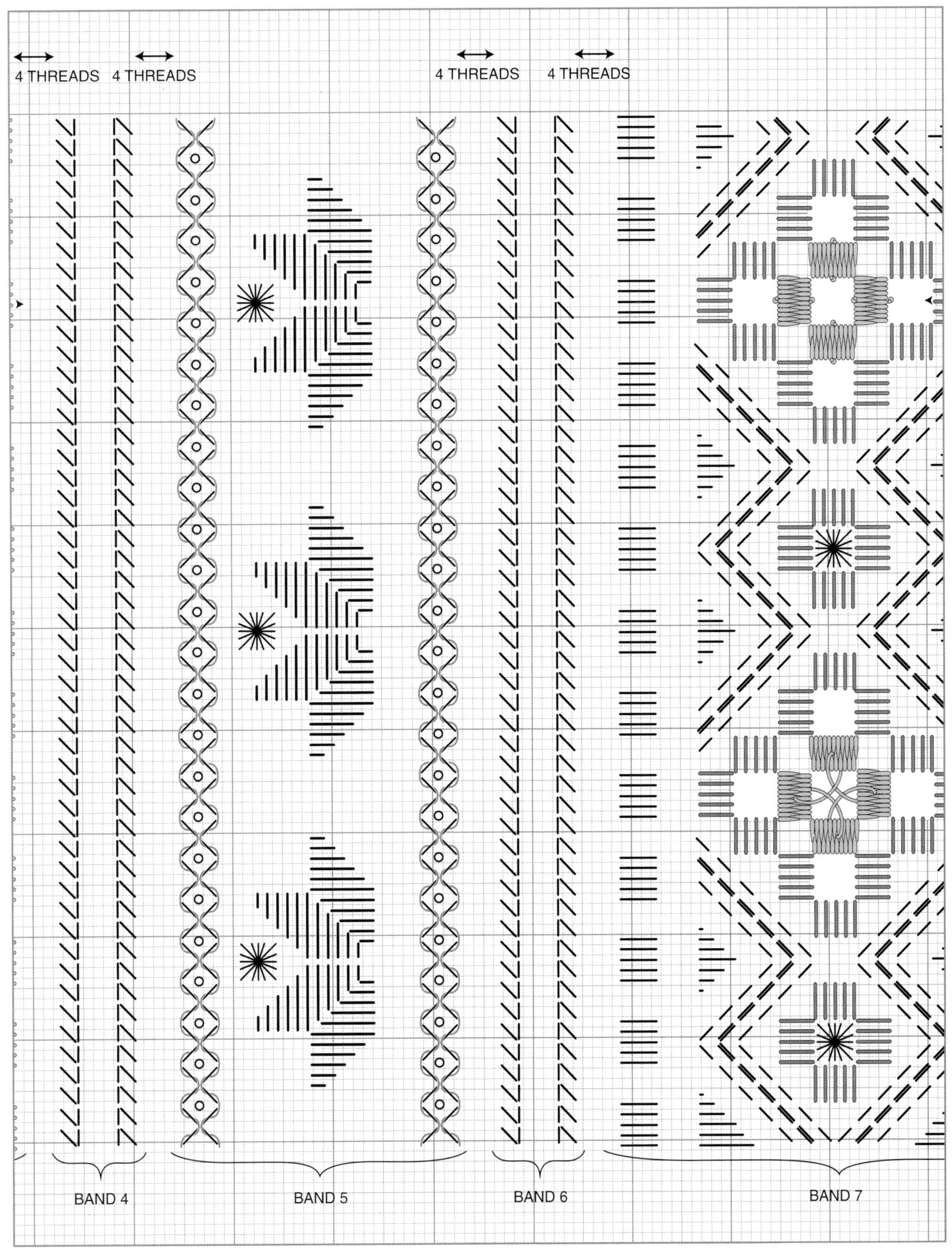
4 THREADS
4 THREADS
4 THREADS
4 THREADS
BAND 4
BAND 5
BAND 6
BAND 7

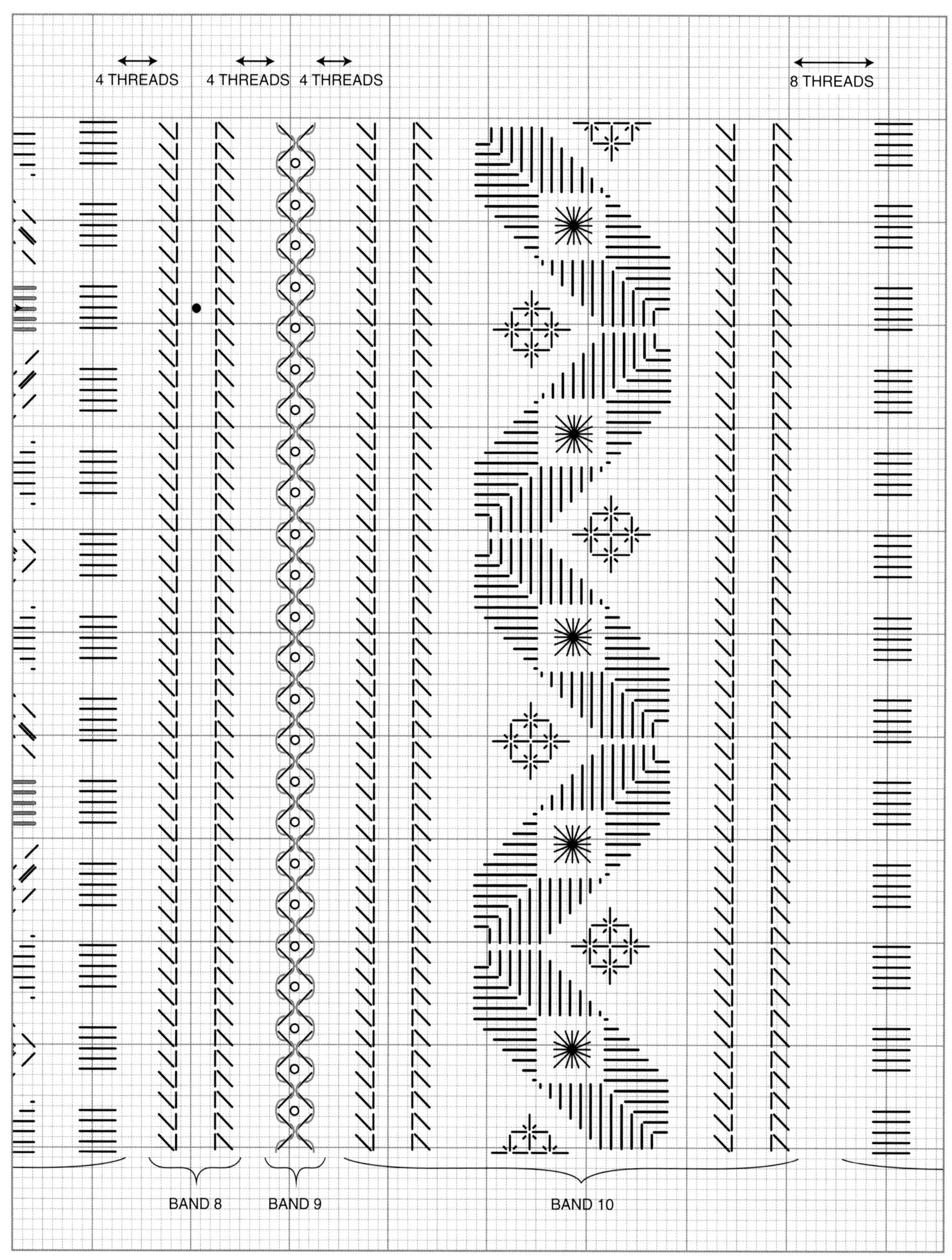
4 THREADS
4 THREADS
4 THREADS
8 THREADS
BAND 8
BAND 9
BAND 10

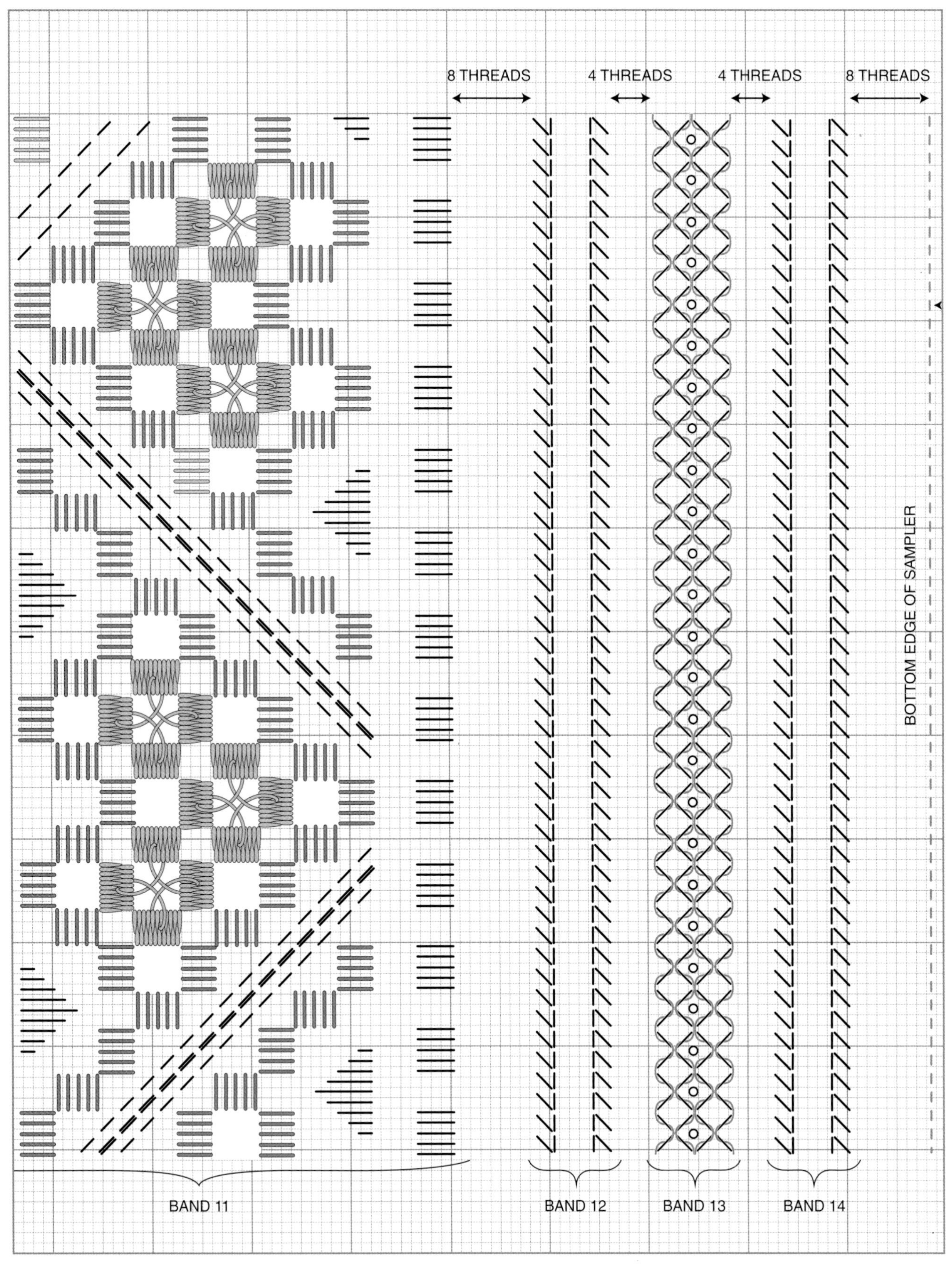
8 THREADS
4 THREADS
4 THREADS
8 THREADS
BOTTOM EDGE OF SAMPLER
BAND 11
BAND 12
BAND 13
BAND 14

'Valentine' Hardanger Heart-Shaped Cushion

This heart cushion brings a message of love and romance, with heart motifs in Hardanger embroidery. Four heart motifs reverse to create a cross at the bottom of the design, sealing it with a kiss! The coloured background fabric, which can be changed to suit any occasion, highlights the delicacy of the small knots. A tasselled cord adds the finishing touch. If preferred, this design could be turned into a herb pillow full of soothing herbs.

Finished size of embroidery:
approximately 18 x 25.5cm (7 x 10in)
Finished size of cushion:
22.9 x 27cm (9 x 10⅝in)

Materials

45cm (18in) square white evenweave linen, 26 threads to the inch

White DMC Coton Perlé No. 8 and No. 12 (1 reel of each)

5 small pearl beads (optional)

Tapestry needle size 24

Fine, sharp-pointed scissors

Pastel-coloured basting cotton

38cm (15in) square red cotton for lining

38cm (15in) square backing fabric, linen or cotton

Heart-shaped cushion pad (or make your own)

Two 51cm (20in) squares of strong cotton fabric, and chosen filling, if making your own cushion

110cm (43in) twisted cord

Tassel 11cm (4½in):

DMC Coton Perlé No. 8 and No. 12

Piece of stiff card (12cm/4¾in) square

Instructions

1 Read and refer to the section on Hardanger techniques and stitches, pages 24-33. Prepare the linen as described. Find the centre line lengthways, measure 20cm (8in) in from the top edge and start your first Kloster block on the centre line at A. Proceed clockwise, following the chart and key on page 104.

2 Establish the first heart motif (see chart on page 106) in the middle at the top of the design and build up the rest of the pattern from this motif. Complete all the Kloster blocks, remembering to check the blocks are lined up in all directions.

3 Complete all the eyelets keeping the holes as even as possible.

4 Stitch the reversed diagonal faggoting.

5 Work the simple star motif and four surrounding eyelets following Fig. 1. Add the beads to the star centres.

Fig. 1

6 Cut the threads from one motif at a time and needleweave the bars, incorporating small French knots (or any other decorative filling of your choice).

7 If necessary, wash carefully, dry and press.

8 If you are making a cushion pad, trace the template, adding 25mm (1in) all round. (Cushion pads should be larger than their covers.) Cut two pieces of strong cotton fabric using the new template. Place right sides together and machine stitch 1cm (⅜in) from the edge leaving an opening on the side for filling. Turn inside out, fill firmly with the stuffing of your choice and then ladderstitch the opening (page 37).

9 Trace the original template again, adding 15mm (½in) seam allowance. Use tracing to cut the lining and backing pieces. Place the embroidery on top of the lining, right side up, and machine stitch together. Place the backing fabric on top of the embroidery, right sides together. Machine stitch the seam, leaving an opening at the point of the heart large enough to take the pad. Clip the curves, turn inside out, insert the cushion pad and ladderstitch the opening.

10 Attach the cord round the cushion (page 42), starting and finishing at the point of the heart, stitching the two ends of cord firmly together.

11 Make a tassel to hide the ends. Take an end of each of your two chosen yarns and wrap as one round your piece of card 60 times, or to your own preferred thickness. Slip a piece of waste thread through the loops at the top to hold the tassel together, and remove from the card by cutting the bottom loops. Pass one side of the tassel over the cord join. Adjust the lengths of the two sides, bind or wrap the tassel (page 58) as required. Discard the waste thread.

12 If you do not want a tassel, start and finish the cord in the middle of the heart shape at the top, make an opening in the seam. Bend the two cords at right angles to each other, push the ends into the opening and stitch securely.

Alternative ideas and suggestions

- Use pearls in the centres of the eyelets.
- Use space-dyed thread for the stitching.
- Insert contrast piping instead of attaching a cord when making up the cushion.

KEY

On the complete chart opposite, each square represents 4 x 4 threads of fabric. On the heart motif chart, each grid line represents one thread of fabric.

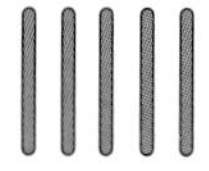

Kloster blocks
DMC Coton Perlé No. 8

Reversed diagonal faggoting
DMC Coton Perlé No. 12

Eyelets
DMC Coton Perlé No. 12

Small star motif
DMC Coton Perlé No. 8

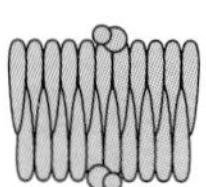

Needleweaving with French knots
DMC Coton Perlé No. 12

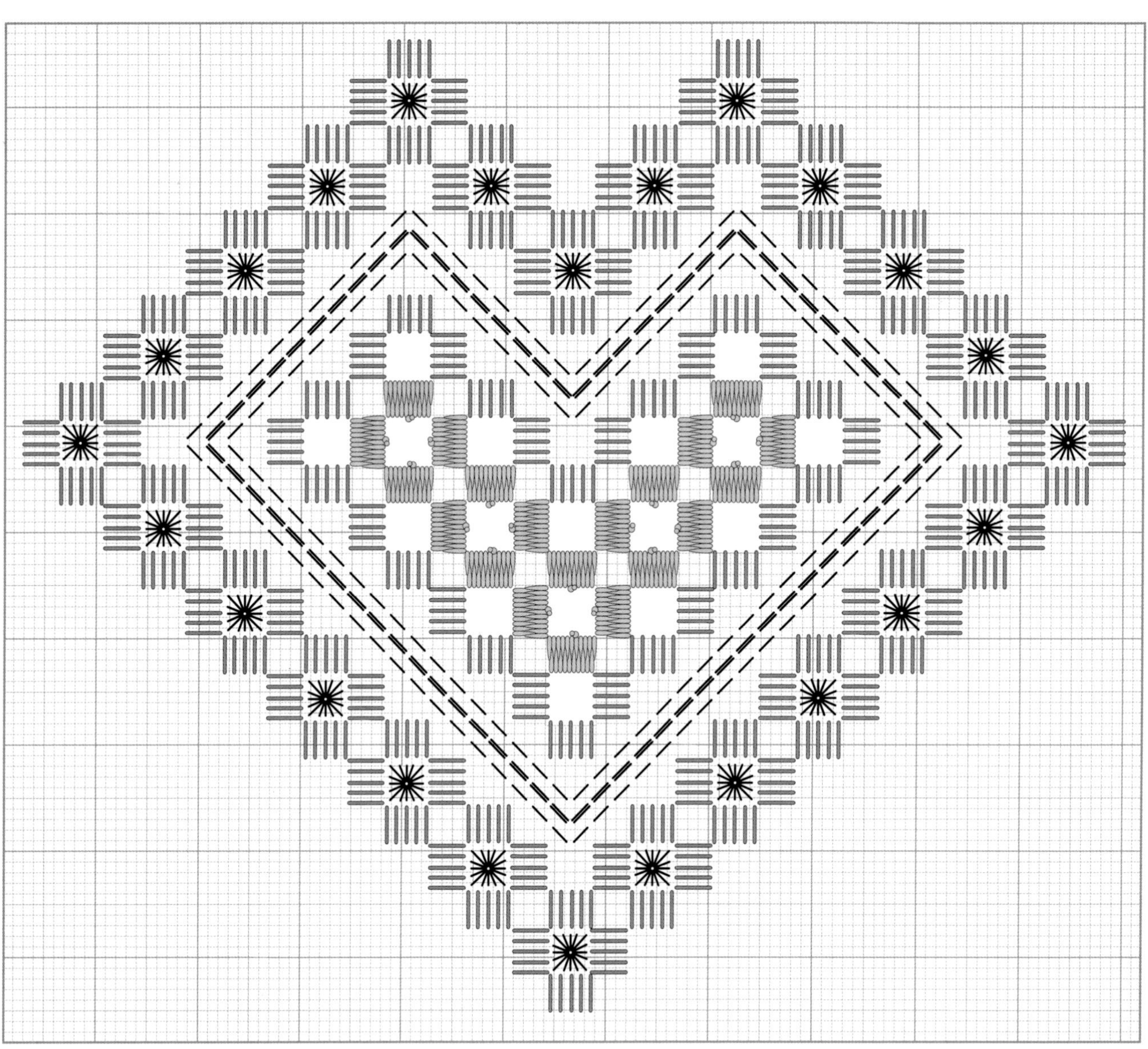

Heart motif

Cushion pad

This is 50% of actual size. Please enlarge on photocopier by 200%. Add 1.3cm (½in) seam allowance.

'Knot Garden' Canvas Work Pin Cushion

■

This design was inspired by a visit to the Château at Villandry in France's Loire Valley. In this wonderful garden, plants jostle in ordered squares and triangles bordered by neat grass verges. The memory has been developed into canvas work embroidery using wool and stranded cotton (floss) in complementary greens and pinks on a pincushion. The 'grass' path is the place for pins so as not to spoil the flower beds! This is a project reminding us of beautiful places and gardens we have visited, and it would be warmly received on any special occasion.

Finished size of pin cushion:
12.5 x 12.5cm (5 x 5in)

Materials

28cm (11in) square antique mono de-luxe canvas, 18 threads to the inch

3 skeins each Appleton crewel wool 355, 354, 353, 756, 941, 943, 945

2 skeins each Anchor stranded cotton (floss) 261

1 skein Anchor stranded cotton (floss) 1021

Small pink beads to match stranded cotton (floss) 1021 (optional)

1.2m (1¼ yd) white cotton tape, 25mm (1in) wide

1.5m (1¾ yd) twisted cord for edging

Tapestry needles size 22 (for the crewel wool) and 24 (for the cotton/floss)

25cm (10in) square wooden frame/artist's canvas stretcher bars

Drawing pins or staple gun

20cm (8in) square cotton backing

2 x 20cm (8in) squares of calico for lining

Instructions

1 Read and refer to the section on canvas work techniques and stitches, pages 8-19. Prepare the canvas and attach to the frame as described. Tack (baste) along the centre lines.

2 Measure 6.5cm (2½in) from the centre point and start stitching at A, following the chart and key. Outline the garden and flower beds with Smyrna cross. Notice that the direction of the top thread of the cross changes as it goes round the square.

3 **Flower bed 1** Fill with reversed cushion stitch and upright cross centre, with a line of back stitches breaking up each square and an upright cross on the intersection.

4 **Flower beds 2, 3, 4 and 7** Filled with eyelet daisies, intersected by double straight cross and outlined with back stitch. Add compensating stitches of half of the double straight cross at the edges.

5 **Flower beds 5 and 6** Stitch with reversed diagonal mosaic forming a square, with a centre Smyrna cross, a broken outline of back stitch and another Smyrna cross on the intersection. Work compensating small crosses at the edges.

6 **Flower bed 8** Centre a square of reversed diagonal mosaic and outline with tent stitch.

7 **Flower bed 9** Fill with reversed mosaic.

8 **Grass path** Work in diagonal satin stitch and mosaic, spotting the mosaic stitches and sewing on the beads as shown on the chart.

9 Stitch a further path of long-armed cross stitch round the Smyrna cross border.

10 Outline with a single row of tent stitch to prevent the canvas showing if your machine line is not straight when you make up the cushion.

11 Work a pale-yellow French knot in the centre of each flower (optional), and stitch the pink beads randomly through the central grass path.

12 Stretch the canvas (page 11).

Making up the pin cushion

1 To make up the pin cushion, cut out the backing piece of fabric. Stitch the two pieces together (right-sides together) just inside the line of tent stitch and turn inside out.

2 To make the filling pad, repeat the process with two pieces of strong calico (the same size as the finished pin cushion). Three-quarters fill the calico bag with sawdust and then carefully ease into the pincushion.

3 Settle the sawdust and then completely fill the calico bag. Securely sew up the opening and then, ladderstitch the pin cushion opening.

4 Attach the cord and tassels as described for the Hardanger heart-shaped cushion on page 101. For the tassels, wrap a single strand of crewel wool twelve times around a piece of card 38mm (1½in) in depth to make a finished tassel of 32mm (1¼in) long.

Alternative ideas and suggestions

- Change the colourway.
- Stitch green beads round the edge as on the yellow pincushion (see page 7).
- Stitch a bead in the centre of each flower.
- Use the design for a box-top pincushion.

The knot garden design has been worked for the top of the box.

KEY

Each grid line represents one thread of canvas

Border
Smyrna cross
Appleton 355 & 354 (1 strand of each)

Flower bed 1
Reversed cushion stitch with upright cross centre
Appleton 943 (2 strands), Anchor 1021 (6 strands)

Flower bed 1
Back stitch outline with upright cross
Anchor 261 (6 strands)

Flower bed 2, 3 & 7
Daisies (alternating) with double straight cross
Appleton 945 & 756 (2 strands), Appleton 941 (2 strands)

Flower bed 4
Daisies (alternating) with double straight cross
Appleton 943 & 945 (2 strands), 756 (2 strands)

Flower beds 2, 3, 4 & 7
Back stitch
Anchor 261 (6 strands)

Flower beds 5 & 6
Reversed diagonal mosaic with Smyrna cross centre
Appleton 943 (2 strands), 261 (6 strands)

Flower bed 5 & 6
Back stitch outline with upright cross
Anchor 262 (6 strands)

Flower bed 8
Reversed diagonal mosaic with Smyrna cross centre
Appleton 943 (2 strands), 261 (6 strands)

Flower bed 9
Reversed mosaic
Appleton 945 (6 strands)

Grass path 10
Diagonal satin stitch
Appleton 353 (2 strands)

Mosaic stitch
Anchor 261 (6 strands)

Mosaic stitch
Appleton 353 & 354 (1 strand of each)

Mosaic stitch
Appleton 353 (2 strands)

Outline Path
Long-armed cross
Appleton 355 & 354 (1 strand of each)

Outline border
Tent stitch
Appleton 355 & 354 (1 strand of each)

3
10
4
6
9
5
7
A

'Forget Me Not' Canvas Work Photo Frame

Capture a memory and border a favourite photograph for posterity with this distinctive and unusual picture frame inspired by Forget-me-nots. The canvas work stitches worked in shades of blue wool are accentuated with shiny stranded cottons (floss). Change the colours to suit your own photograph – perhaps bottle green, wine red or black and grey.

Finished size of design:
21.5 x 25.5cm (8½ x 10in)

Materials

38 x 41cm (15 x 16in) antique mono de-luxe canvas, 18 threads to the inch

1oz hank Appleton crewel wool 749, 747

3 skeins Appleton crewel wool 744,

3 skeins Anchor stranded cotton (floss) 136, 150

Tapestry needles sizes 22 (wool) and 24 (cotton)

46 x 61cm (18 x 24in) roller frame

Cardboard

Pins

Fabric adhesive

Instructions

1 Read and refer to the section on canvas work techniques and stitches, pages 8-19. Prepare the canvas and attach it to the frame as described. Mark the centre of the canvas with a small dot.

2 Following the chart and the key, begin stitching at A, 12.7cm (5in) from the centre. Using double straight cross, first work the basic outline of large diamonds to establish the pattern. Note the direction of the top crosses and that two colours are used. Link the framework with the smaller diamond pattern.

3 Outline the small diamond shapes with back stitch using stranded cotton (floss). Fill in the small diamond with tent stitch worked in one direction.

4 Work the central flower in the large diamonds over eight threads (Fig. 1). Fill in the areas around the flower with two-directional tent stitch. Tuck the tent stitch underneath the arm of the double straight cross at the edge.

Fig. 1

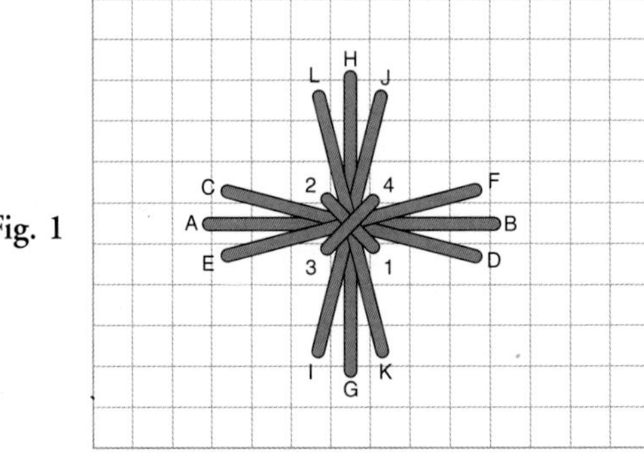

5 Complete the background with two-directional diagonal mosaic stripe, using stranded cotton (floss) 150 between each line of mosaic stitches. On the edges and centre line work a small compensating stitch but keep going with whichever thread you are using, to keep the pattern correct.

6 Work two rows of tent stitch round the outer edge and one row of long-armed cross round the inner edge.

7 Stretch the canvas. Once mounted take the finished piece to a professional framer.

Making the Photograph Mount

1 Cut a piece of cardboard size of the embroidery and cut a window to fit the centre. With the embroidery face down on a clean surface, position the window mount.

2 Insert pins into the edge of the card to secure. Fold over the canvas, trimming excess bulk at the corners. Apply fabric adhesive to the canvas and stick to the card. Trim canvas to 25mm (1in).

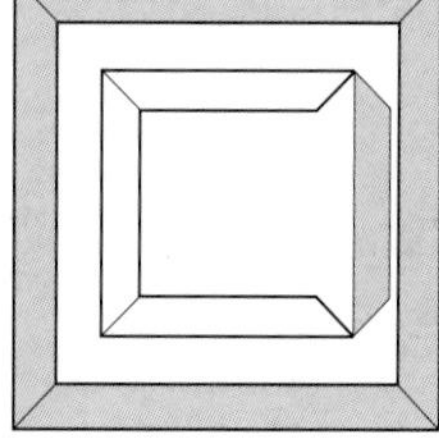

Fig. 2

3 Cut out the centre of the canvas, snipping carefully into the corners. Apply adhesive and carefully fold canvas back, taking care to make neat corners. The edging of long-armed cross helps to cover and should be sitting astride the edge of the window frame, so that no canvas shows from the front.

KEY

Each grid line represents one thread of canvas.

Large diamond outline
Double straight cross
(underneath cross)
Appleton 747
2 strands
(top cross)
Appleton 744
2 strands

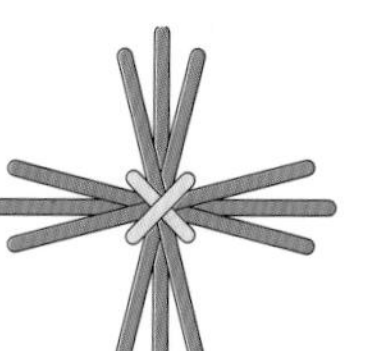

Central flower
(underneath cross)
Appleton 744
2 strands
(top cross)
Anchor 136
6 strands

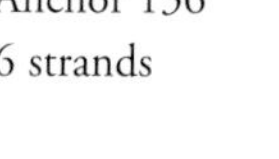

Tent stitch (two directional)
Appleton 747
2 strands

Smaller diamond outline
Double straight cross
(underneath cross)
Appleton 747
2 strands
(top cross)
Anchor 136
6 strands

Outline back stitch
Anchor 136
6 strands

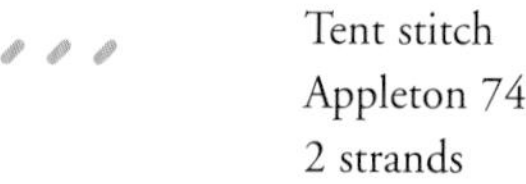

Tent stitch
Appleton 747
2 strands

Background
Diagonal mosaic
Appleton 749
2 strands
with diagonal tent
Anchor 150
6 strands

Outline tent
Appleton 749
2 strands

Inner line, long-armed cross
Appleton 749
2 strands

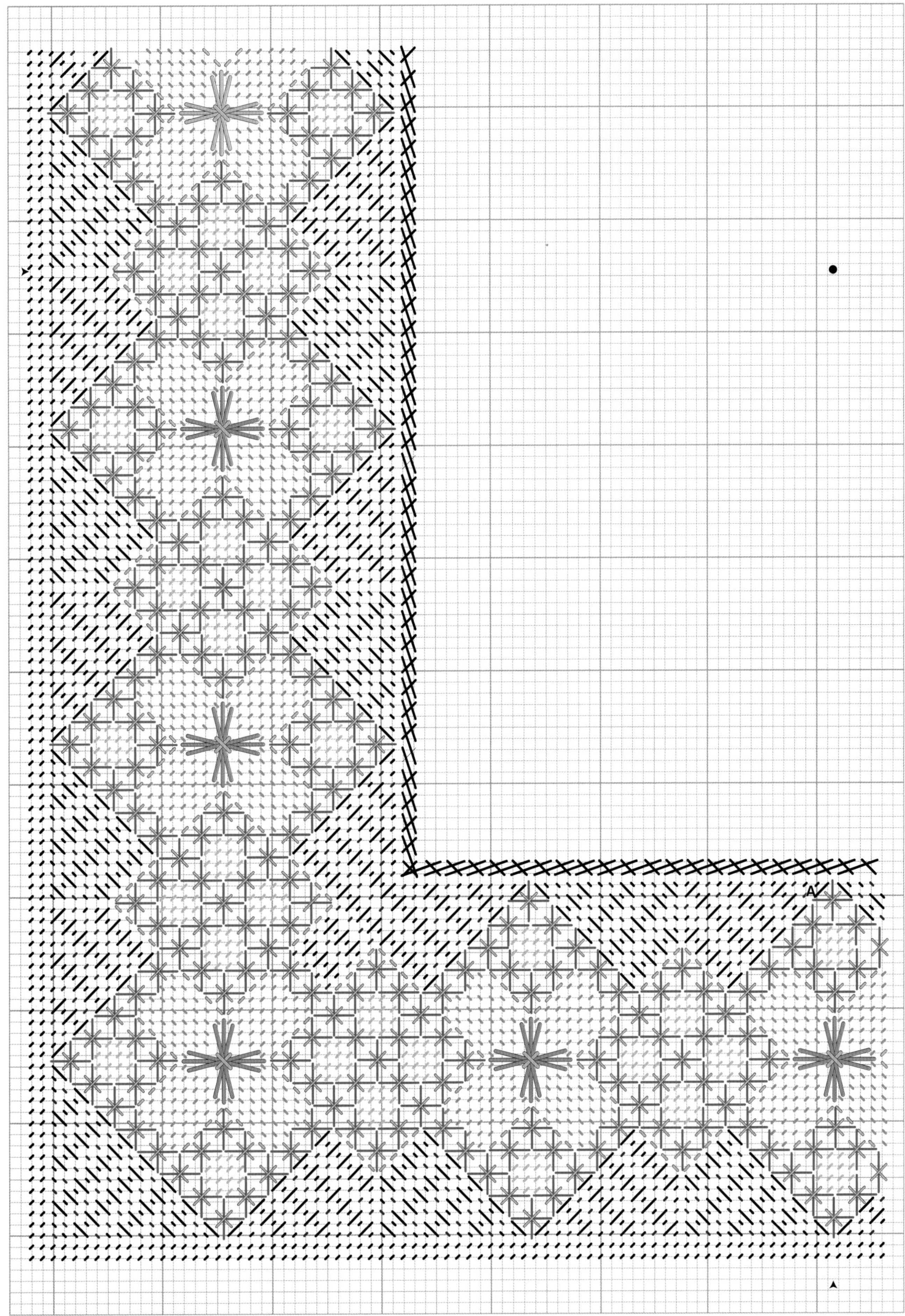

CHAPTER 5

CHRISTMAS

This chapter evokes all that is Christmas in sparkling white, bright reds, greens, blues and touches of glittering gold. The projects using canvas work and Hardanger embroidery techniques include:

A cake band in Hardanger embroidery dresses up your cake for Christmas.

A traditional but formal stocking in canvas work boasting all manner of surprises.

A Hardanger heart-shaped Christmas decoration.

A Christmas tree hanging in Hardanger embroidery worked in festive colours to decorate any tree with style.

'Great Expectations' Hardanger Cake Band

◆

This unconventional cake band in vibrant Christmas colours is a stunning addition to the tea table and, as it is washable, it will definitely return each year to be part of your family tradition. A symbolic cross of eyelets and Kloster blocks forms the basis of the design, with open-work centres and an outline edging of eyelets and buttonhole stitch. Stitch as many repeats as necessary to fit your cake.

Finished width: *6cm (2⅜in)*
Length of repeat: *8.2cm (3¼in)*

Materials

Red evenweave fabric, 27/28 threads per inch to the size required. Allow 6.5cm (2½in) around the design.

DMC Coton Perlé No. 8, Green 910 (1 reel)

DMC Coton Perlé No. 12, Red 666 (1 reel)

Tapestry needle size 24

Fine, sharp-pointed scissors

Pale-coloured basting thread

Instruction

1 Refer to the section on Hardanger stitches, pages 24-33. Prepare the linen as described.

2 Following the chart and the key, start stitching at A on the centre line, 6.5cm (2½in) from the right-hand end of the fabric. Follow Route 1, working the Kloster blocks to establish the design.

3 Follow Route 2 to stitch the inner Kloster blocks. Work the small square centre of Kloster blocks, taking your starting and finishing threads through the back of the stitches to secure.

4 Stitch the required number of repeats.

5 Outline the whole design with buttonhole stitch edging, and work the four uncompleted Kloster blocks on each side of the design as you go.

6 Work the eyelets with holes the same size.

7 Complete the reversed diagonal faggoting stitch in each repeat.

8 Following the chart, cut the threads one repeat at a time to form the central grid for needleweaving.

9 Once the embroidery has been completed wash it carefully, if necessary, before cutting the embroidery away from the fabric, remembering to cut from the back.

10 Treat the embroidery like a paper cake band, and pin carefully to the cake.

KEY

Each grid line represents one thread of fabric. Turn book and work embroidery from right to left. Use one strand of DMC Coton Perlé throughout.

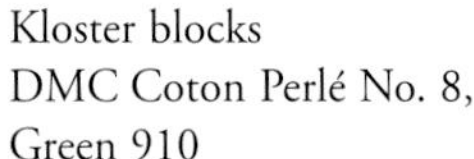

Kloster blocks
DMC Coton Perlé No. 8,
Green 910

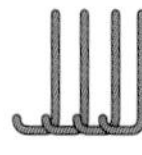

Buttonhole stitch edging
DMC Coton Perlé No. 8,
Green 910

Eyelets in Kloster blocks/edging
DMC Coton Perlé No. 12,
Red 666

Central Kloster block motif
DMC Coton Perlé No. 8,
Green 910
with eyelet
DMC Coton Perlé No. 12,
Red 666

Reversed diagonal faggoting
DMC Coton Perlé No. 12,
Red 666

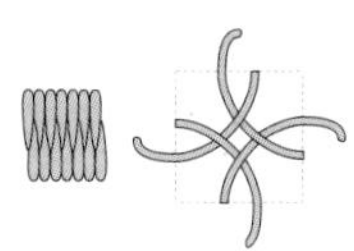

Needleweaving and dove's eye filling
DMC Coton Perlé No. 12,
Red 666

A
B
ROUTE 1
ROUTE 2
EACH END
REPEAT OF 96 THREADS

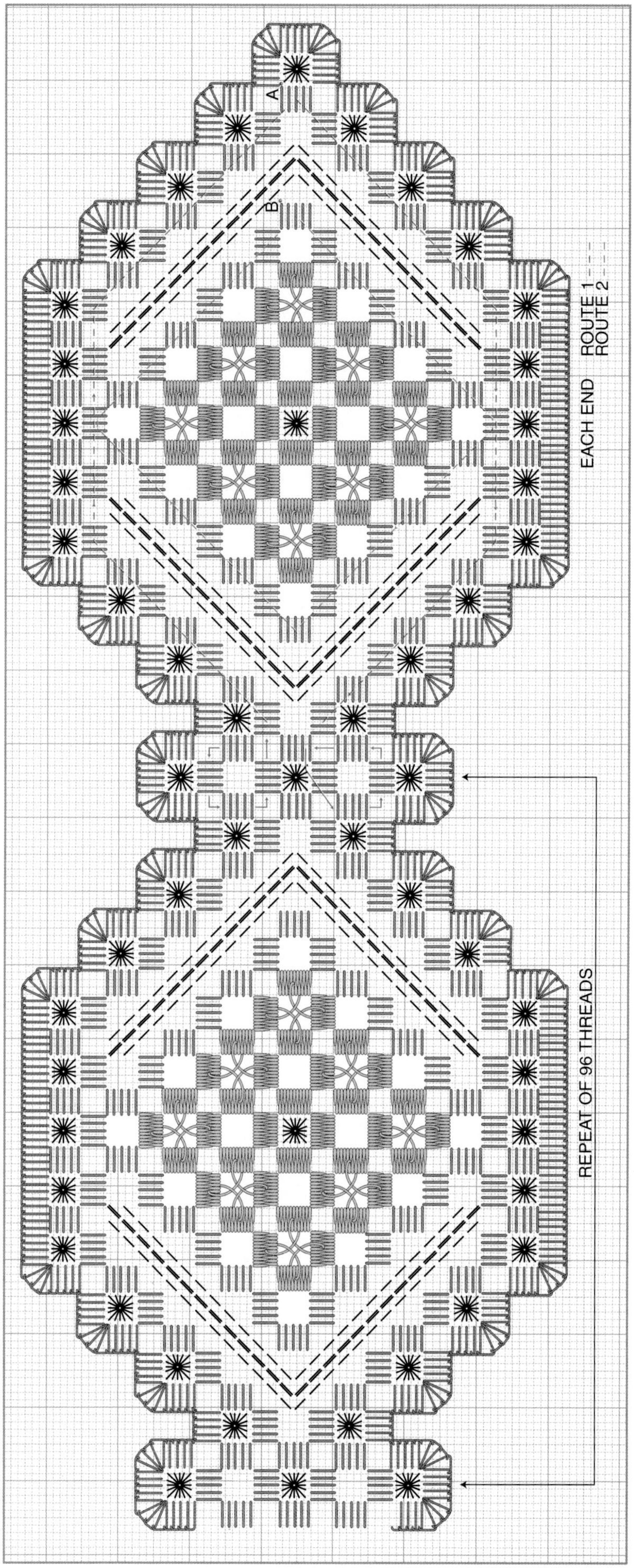

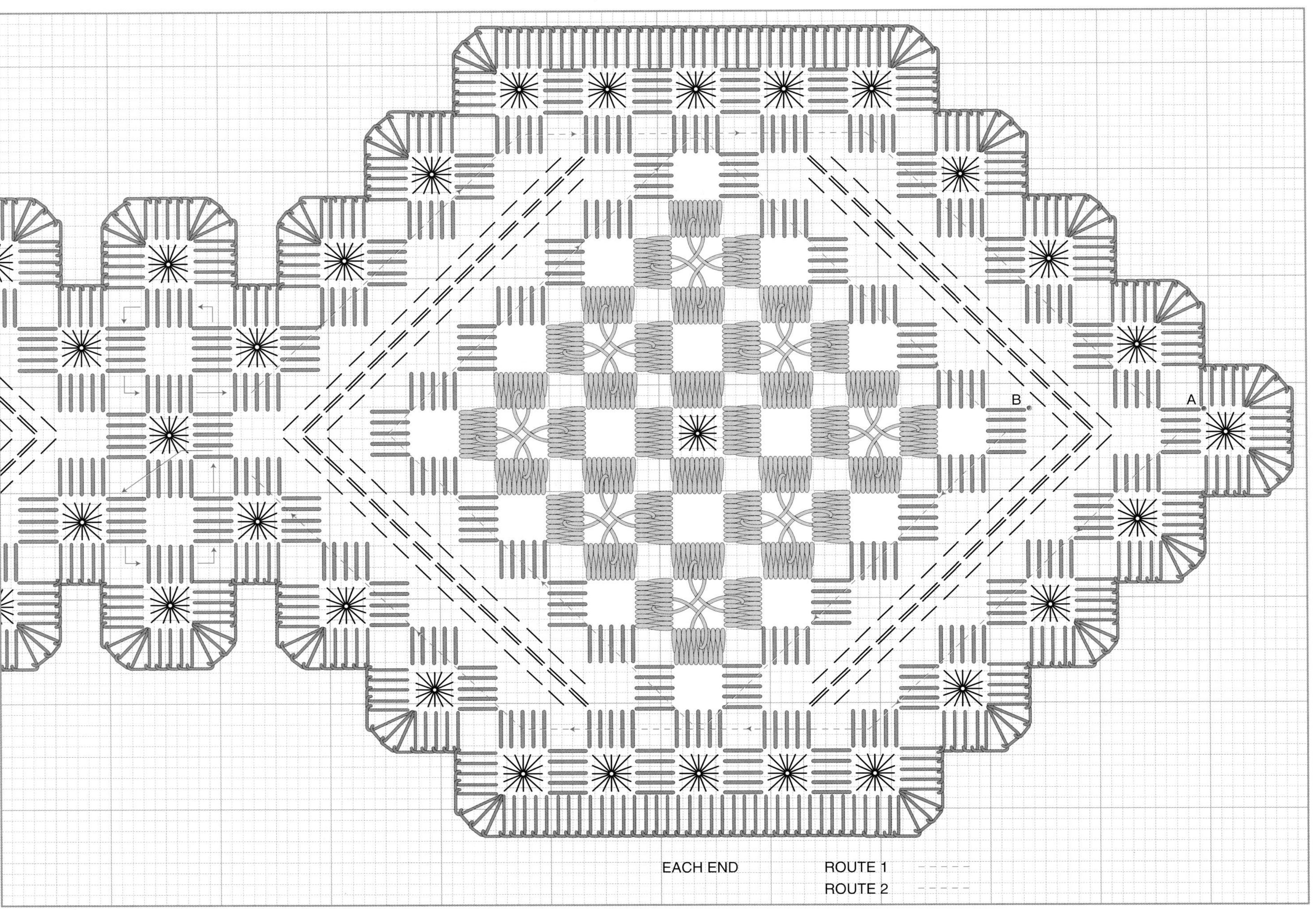
A
B
EACH END
ROUTE 1
ROUTE 2

'Presents' Canvas Work Christmas Stocking

With Christmas being a time for celebration and giving, here is a traditional Christmas stocking to dazzle friends and family. Admire it as a fireside decoration, or fill it with small presents. The design of excitingly wrapped boxes worked in a variety of stitches is placed on a discreet background tartan which makes it possible to enjoy and display the stocking on occasions other than Christmas. Canvas work stitches combined with stranded cotton (floss) and metallic threads are worked in vibrant colours to show up on the tent stitch background. In this design, some piles of presents are reversed to maximize the effect of the stitches.

Finished size of canvas design:
approximately 51 x 31cm (20 x 12in)

Materials

44 x 66cm (17 x 26in) antique mono de-luxe canvas, 14 threads to the inch

Tartan background:

1oz hank Appleton crewel wool 465, 438, 835

4 skeins Appleton crewel wool 852, 503

Presents:

3 skeins Appleton crewel wool 447, 428, 824

1 skein Anchor stranded cotton (floss) 46, 228, 134

1 reel Madeira metallic No. 8 gold 8014

Tapestry needles sizes 22 and 24

2m (2½yd) twisted cord for edging

38 x 58cm (15 x 23in) woollen backing fabric or cotton needlecord and matching thread

2 pieces x 38 x 58cm (15 x 23in) lining fabric

2.5m (2¾yd) white cotton tape, 25mm (1in) wide

61cm (24in) roller frame

Instructions

1 Read and refer to the section on canvas work techniques and stitches, pages 8-19. Prepare the canvas and attach to the frame as described. Tack (baste) along the centre lines.

2 Measure 17cm (6¾in) down from the top edge and start at point Z, 10.5cm (4in) to the left of the centre line. Following the chart and the key begin with the line of long-armed cross stitch.

3 From this first row establish the dominant red lines running through the tartan, working the first groups of presents as you come to them. I suggest stitching 6-8cm

(2½-3in) of the red grid then completing the presents and background tartan in that area. This will help to avoid miscounting and make it interesting to sew. The presents are worked in crewel wool and the ribbons are worked in stranded cotton (floss) and gold metallic thread.

4 Work the stocking top 'rib' with rows of long-armed cross and tent stitch. Edge the top with a single row of tent stitch to prevent the canvas showing if your machine line is not straight when making up.

5 Add bows using the metallic thread or use embroidery stitches of your own choice.

6 Stretch the canvas.

Making up the Stocking

1 Pin the backing fabric to the canvas, right sides together. Tack (baste). Machine stitch round the stocking, as close to the stitchery as possible, leaving the top open. Trim seams to 12mm (½in) and overlock to strengthen. Bring top raw edge over to the wrong side and hem down. Snip curves and turn right sides out.

2 Cut out two pieces of lining to the same size as the stocking. Machine stitch them together, leaving the top open. Slip lining into stocking, pushing it right down to the toe. Catch with a few small hand stitches to prevent it pulling out. Turn a hem at the top of the lining and hem or ladderstitch to the top of the canvas stocking, leaving a small opening on the side edges for tucking in the cord ends.

3 Attach the cord (page 42) and make a loop in one continuous line. Tuck one cord end down a side seam and secure with a few stitches. Stitch the cord round the stocking top, leave enough cord to form a loop, continue down the side, round the toe and up the other side, to tuck down the other end of the cord in the opposite side edge (Fig. 1). Secure with stitching. Stitch the two sides of the loop together at the seam edge to strengthen.

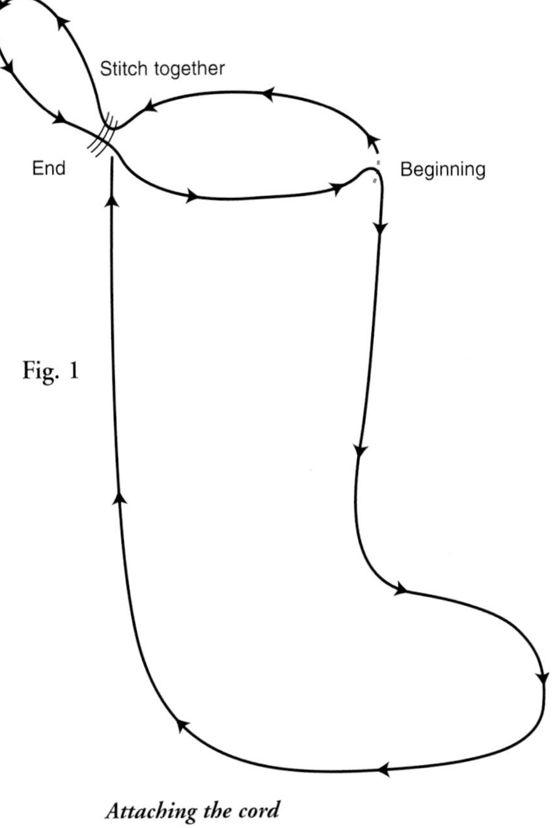

Attaching the cord

Alternative ideas and suggestions

- Add tassels, bobbles or a garter 'flash' on the edge of the stocking rib using any leftover crewel wool.
- Add clusters of beads for bows.
- Insert initials or a name instead of the stocking top rib and surround with tent stitch.
- Personalize the boxes with couched thread initials over the stitches.
- Introduce your own choice of canvas work stitches to interpret the presents.

KEY

Present group 1
On the tartan background chart opposite, each square represents one tent stitch. On the complete stocking chart on p. 129, each grid line represents one thread of canvas.

Rice stitch
Appleton 428 & 824
2 strands of each

Ribbon
Back stitch
Anchor 46 & 228
6 strands

Tent stitch
Madeira gold metallic
1 strand

Present group 2 & 2R (reversed)
Box A
Reversed mosaic stitch
Appleton 428
2 strands

Upright cross stitch
Appleton 447
2 strands

Ribbon
Long armed cross stitch
Anchor 228
6 strands

Tent stitch
Madeira gold metallic
1 strand

Box B
Upright cross stitch
Appleton 824
2 strands

Ribbon
Back stitch
Anchor 46
6 strands
Madeira gold metallic
1 strand

Box C
Mosaic stitch
Appleton 447
3 strands

Ribbon
Tent stitch
Anchor 134
6 strands
Madeira gold metallic
1 strand

Box D
Diagonal satin stitch
Appleton 428
2 strands

Tent stitch
Appleton 428
3 strands

Ribbons
Long-armed cross stitch
Anchor 46
6 strands

Tent stitch
Madeira gold metallic
1 strand

Box E
Rice stitch
Appleton 824 & 447
2 strands of each

Ribbon
Diagonal satin stitch
Anchor 134
6 strands

Back stitch
Madeira gold metallic
1 strand

Present group 3 & 3R (reversed)
Box A
Double stitch with small crosses
Appleton 447
2 strands
Appleton 428 & 824
2 strands of each

Ribbons
Diagonal satin stitch
Anchor 228
6 strands

Tent stitch
Madeira gold metallic
1 strand

Box B
Reversed mosaic stitch
Appleton 284
3 strands

Ribbons
Long-armed cross stitch
Anchor 46
6 strands

Back stitch
Madeira gold metallic
1 strand

Box C
Mosaic stitch
Appleton 428
3 strands

Ribbons
Tent stitch
Anchor 134
6 strands

Tent stitch
Madeira gold metallic
1 strand

Box D
Reversed mosaic
Appleton 447
2 strands

Upright cross stitch
Appleton 428
2 strands

Ribbons
Tent stitch
Anchor 134
6 strands

Back stitch
Madeira gold metallic
1 strand

Present 4
Mosaic stitch
Appleton 428
3 strands

Ribbon
Tent stitch
Anchor 46
6 strands

Tent stitch
Madeira gold metallic
1 strand

Present 5
Rice stitch
Appleton 447
2 strands

Ribbons
Long-armed cross stitch
Anchor 134
6 strands

Back stitch
Madeira gold metallic
1 strand

Present 6
Mosaic
Appleton 428
3 strands

Ribbon
Tent stitch
Anchor 46
6 strands

Tent stitch
Madeira gold metallic
1 strand

Present 6R (reversed)
reversed Mosaic stitch
Appleton 447
3 strands

Ribbon
Tent stitch
Anchor 228
6 strands

Tent stitch
Madeira gold metallic
1 strand

Tartan background
Tent stitch
Appleton 465
3 strands
Appleton 852
3 strands
Appleton 503
3 strands
Appleton 438
3 strands
Appleton 835
3 strands

Stocking top rib
Long-armed cross stitch
Appleton 852 & 835
3 strands of each

Tent stitch
Appleton 852 & 835
3 strands of each

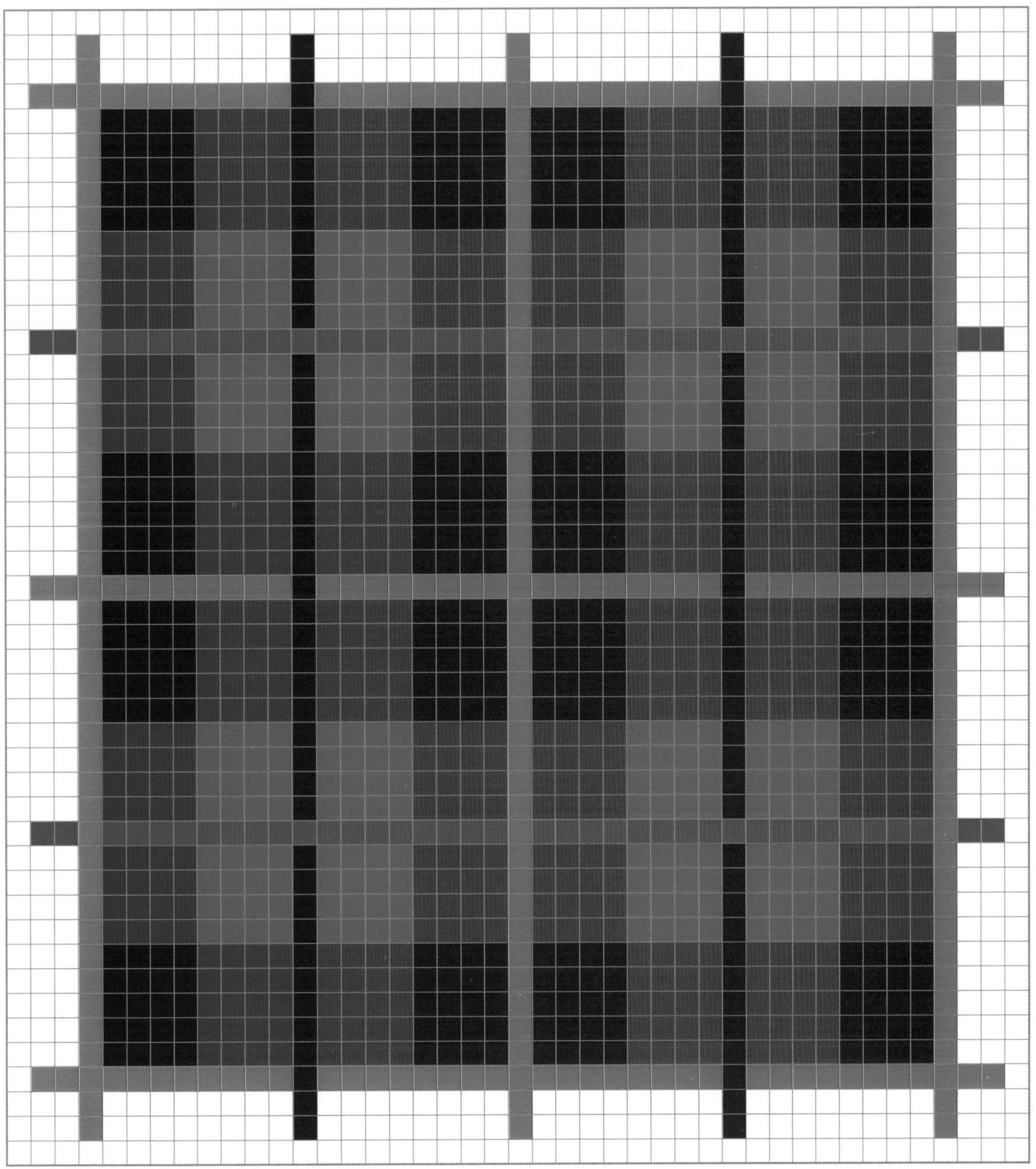

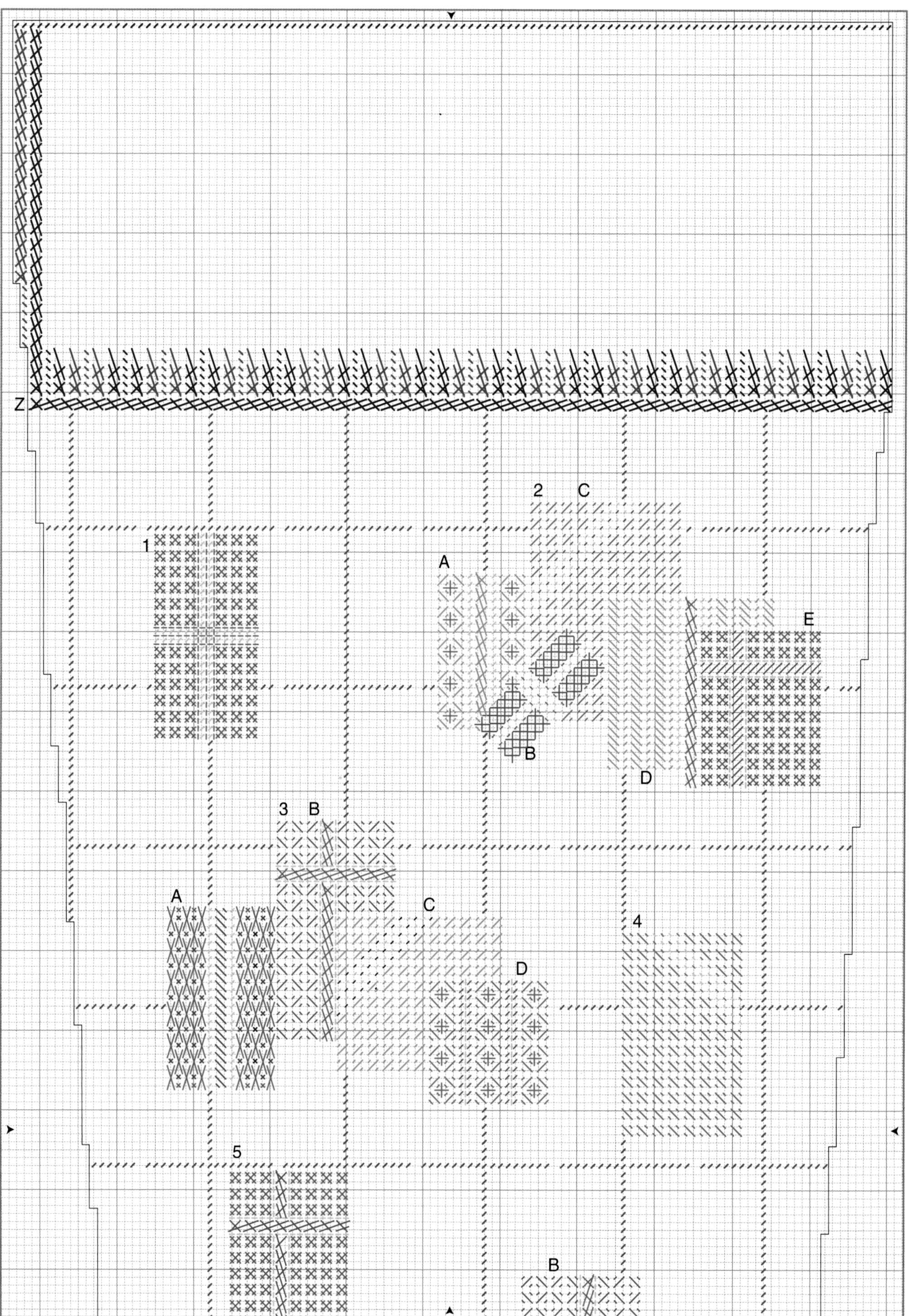
Z
2
C
1
A
E
B
D
3
B
A
C
4
D
5
B

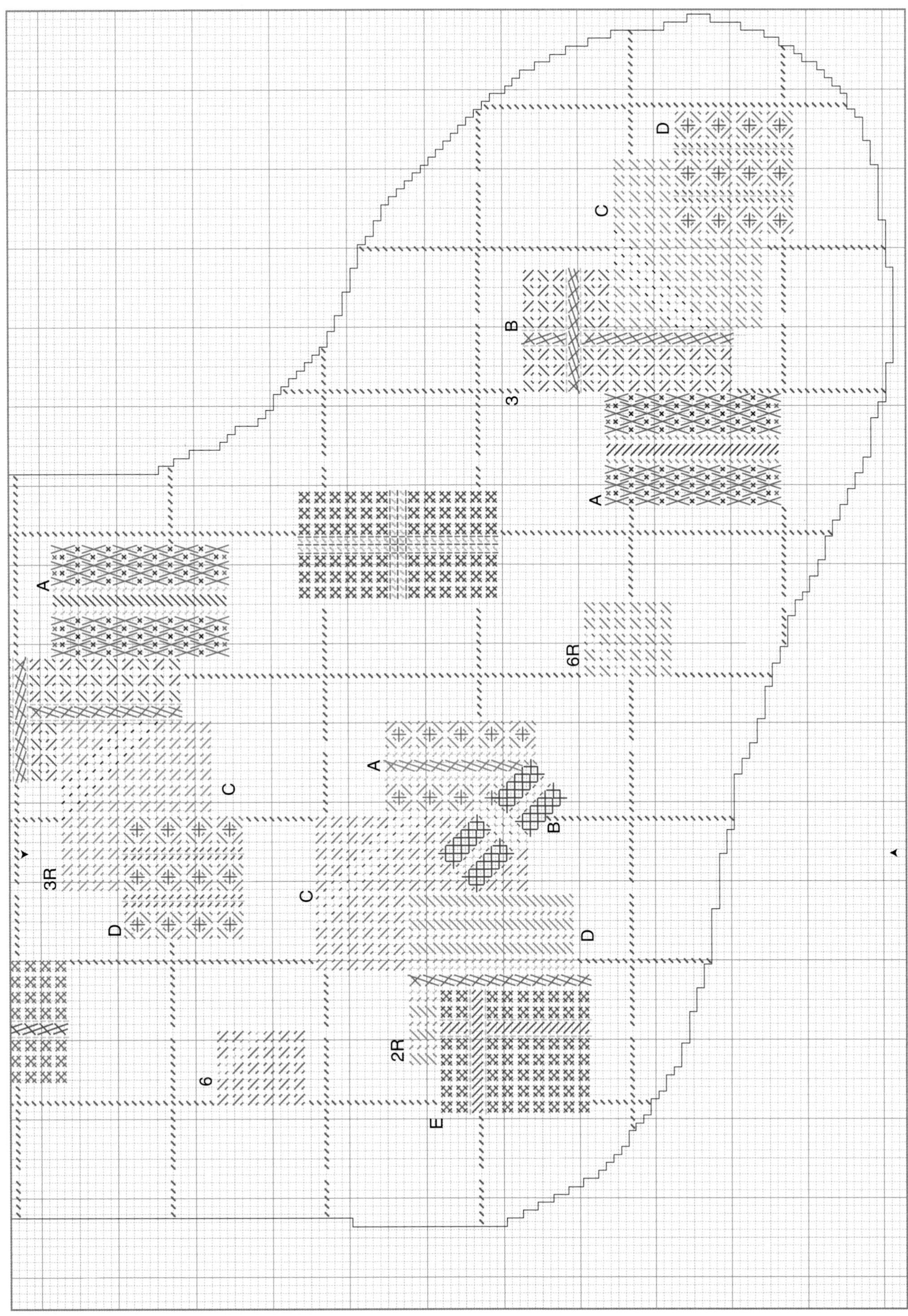
A
A
A
B
B
C
C
C
D
D
D
E
3
3R
6
6R
2R

'Hearts' Hardanger Pot-Pourri Sachet

Savour the smells of Christmas – spicy cinnamon and orange or fresh pine – with this delightful pot-pourri hanging sachet. With time at a premium over the festive season, its small size and simplicity makes this decoration ideal for making and giving. The design is based on the heart design used for the Valentine cushion, with a contrasting backing providing an extra edge of Kloster blocks. It can be varied in many ways to make a selection of unusual and complementary decorations – it could even double up for a Valentine's day present. The instructions below are for the red-and-white sachet with the two red heart beads. The charts offer two variations.

Finished size: *13.5 x 12.5cm (5¼ x 5⅜in)*

Materials

25cm (10in) square Zweigart Lugana red evenweave fabric, 25 threads to the inch for backing fabric

20cm (8in) square Zweigart Lugana white evenweave fabric, 25 threads to the inch for the front fabric

DMC Coton Perlé No. 8, Red 666 (1 reel)

DMC Coton Perlé No. 12, White and Red 666 (1 reel of each)

Tapestry needle size 24

Fine, sharp-pointed scissors

30cm (12in) red satin ribbon, 1.5mm wide

Few red, gold or white pearl beads (optional)

2 small red heart-shaped beads

Beading needle if attaching beads

10 x 9cm (4 x 3½in) red fabric for backing

Tacking (basting) thread

Invisible thread

Small sachet of pot pourri

Instructions

1 Read and refer to the section on Hardanger techniques and stitches, pages 24-33. Prepare the linen as described, marking the centre line lengthways. The fabric allowance is quite generous for easier handling.

2 Following the chart and the key, start stitching on the white evenweave at A, 7.5cm (3in) up from the bottom edge, on the centre line. Establish the basic shape of Kloster blocks, and work the inner Kloster blocks.

3 Outline the whole design with buttonhole stitch edging, keeping an even tension.

4 Work the reversed diagonal faggoting and eyelets. Try to keep the holes the same size.

5 Cut the threads away from the inner part of the design and needleweave the bars with dove's eye filling.

6 On the red evenweave, work the outline of Kloster blocks following the second chart on page 136, starting at A. Outline with the buttonhole stitch edging and eyelets.

7 Cut the embroidery away from the background fabric (page 32).

8 Cut a small piece of red fabric to back the white heart and stitch in place. Thread ribbon through the eyelets and attach the beads on the embroidery.

9 Centre the white heart on the red heart and backstitch together along the line of buttonhole stitches, using invisible thread and leaving an opening at the top. Carefully push in the pouch of pot pourri.

10 Attach a loop of thread at the top and hang two red heart-shaped beads from the bottom.

Alternative ideas and suggestions

- Change the colourways.
- Space-dye evenweave fabric and use contrasting or matching threads.
- Use gold thread for the embroidery.
- Change the filling stitch.
- Vary the type of tassel/beads to hang from the bottom (see the white sachet on page 133).
- As you form the dove's eye filling, thread a bead on each loop.
- Make two or three sachets and link them together to decorate a wall.

Key

Use a single strand of DMC Coton Perlé throughout. Each grid line represents one line of fabric.

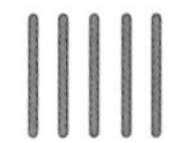

Front piece of fabric
Kloster blocks
DMC Coton Perlé No. 8, White

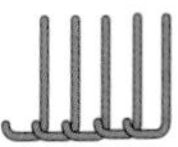

Blanket stitch edging
DMC Coton Perlé No. 8, White

Eyelets in Kloster Blocks/edging
DMC Coton Perlé No. 12, White

Reversed diagonal fagotting
DMC Coton Perlé No. 12, White

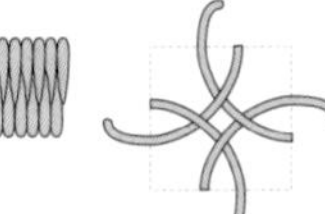

Needleweaving and dove's eye filling
DMC Coton Perlé No. 12, White

Backing piece of fabric
Kloster blocks
DMC Coton Perlé No. 8, Red 666

Blanket stitch edging
DMC Coton Perlé No. 8, Red 666

Eyelets
DMC Coton Perlé No. 12, Red 666

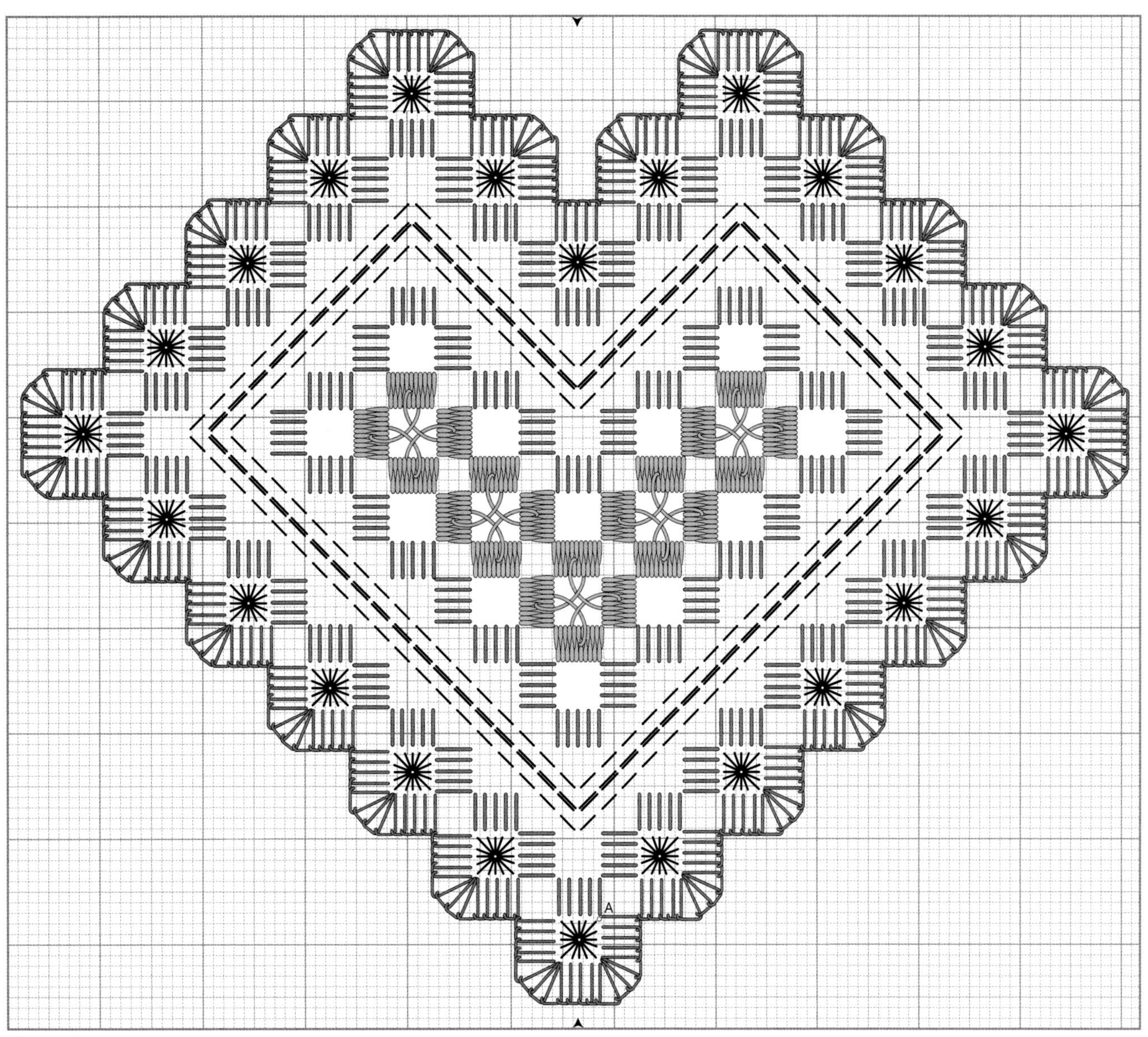

Front design

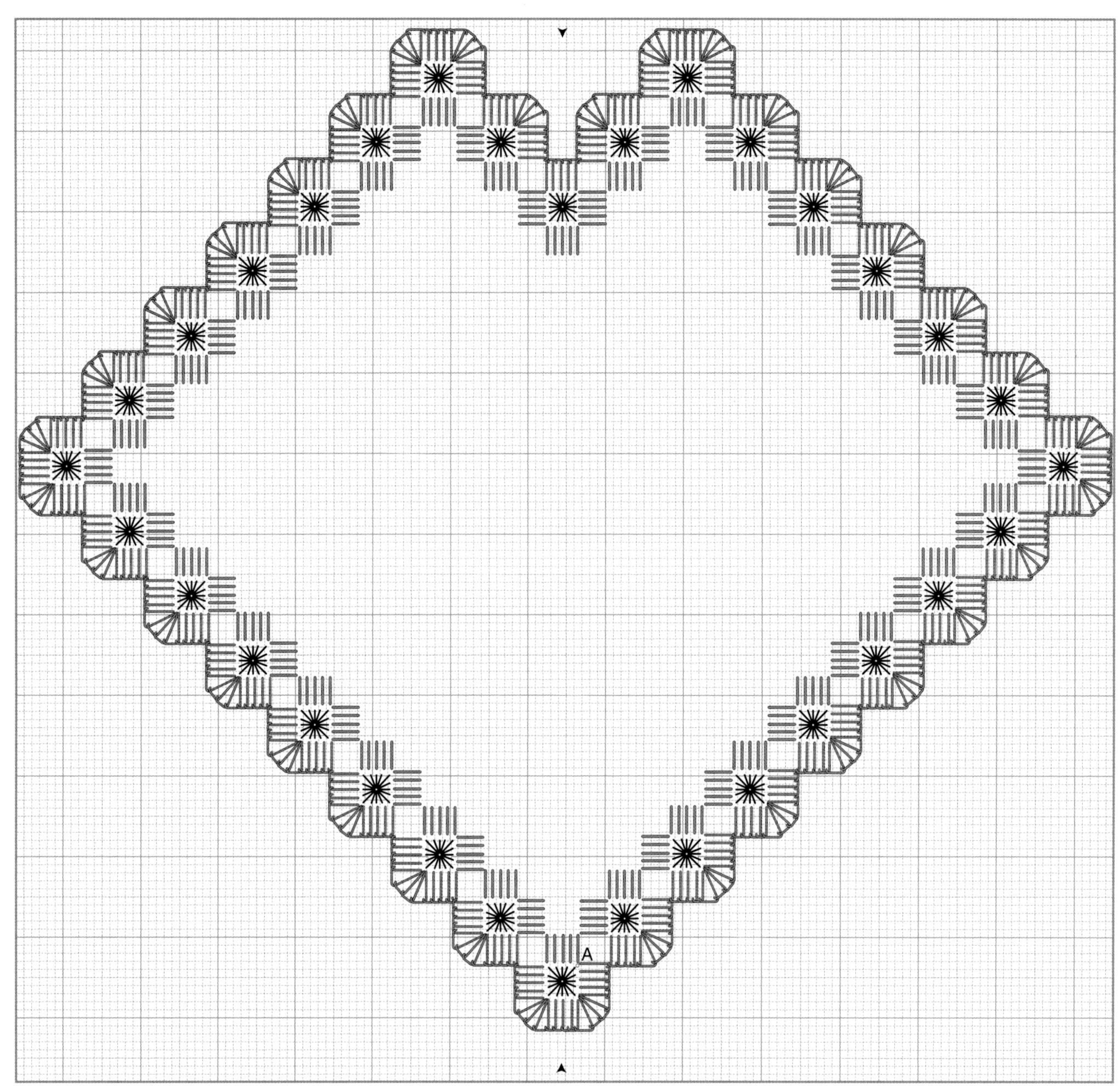

Backing piece

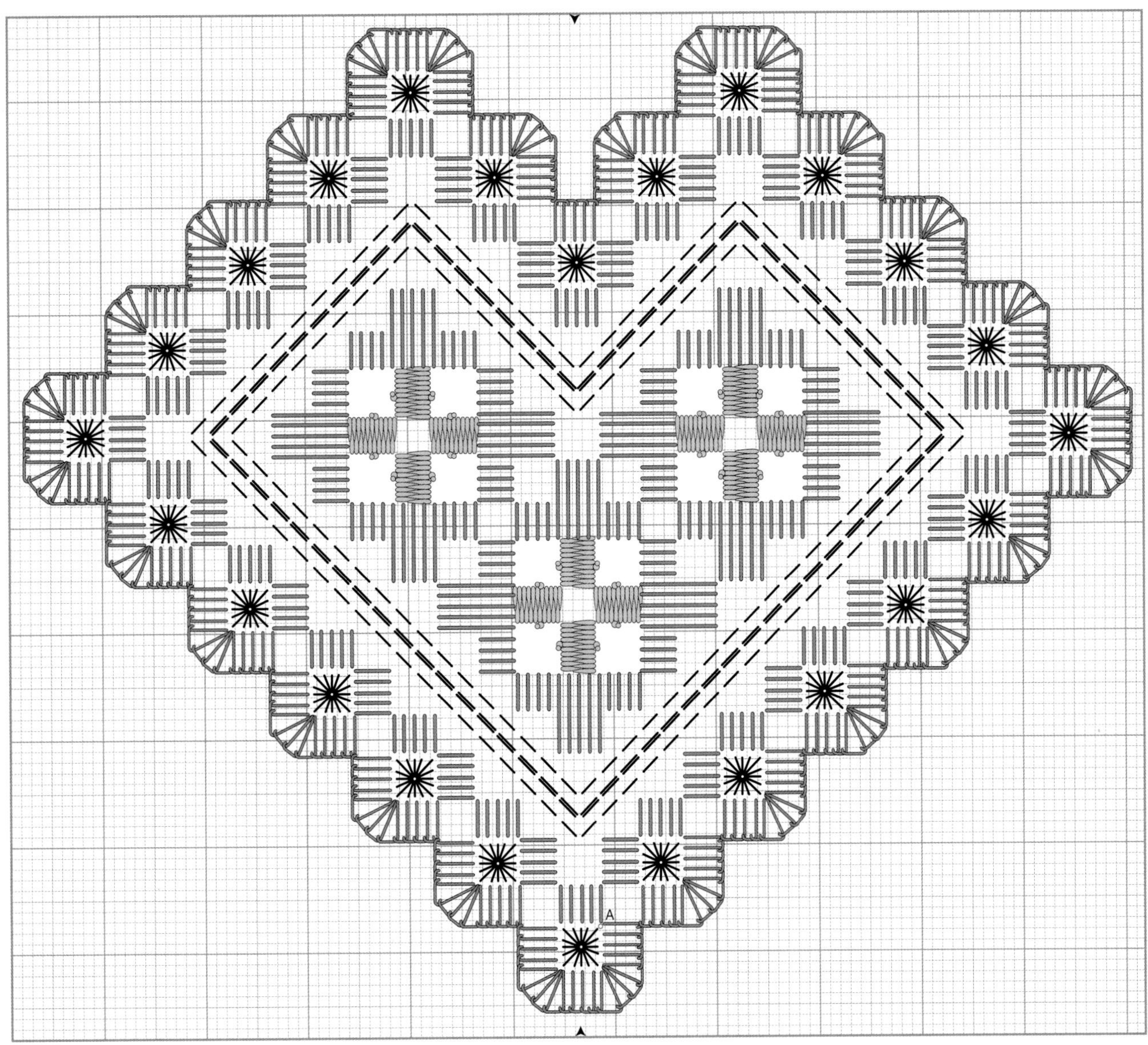

Alternative design for white Hardanger pot pourri sachet

Interpret the chart referring to this project and the section on Hardanger techniques and stitches (pages 24-33). Use the backing outline on page 136.

'Trees'
Hardanger Tree Decoration

These appealing embroidered decorations will be hung on a tree or mantlepiece year after year, whether you make them for yourself or as a present. They are simply worked in a few Hardanger stitches on evenweave fabric, with sparkling gold or silver beads to make them glint. Two or more could be linked together to make a wall or fireside decoration. And to make your own unique designs, you could add different decorative fillings, change the type of tassel, use space-dyed thread, or change the colourways – perhaps green and gold or silver and blue.

Finished size: *10 x 6cm (4 x 2⅜in)*

Materials

18cm (7in) square of Zweigart Lugana red evenweave fabric, 25 threads to the inch

DMC Coton Perlé No. 8, Red 666 (red tree) or Green 699 (green tree) (1 reel of each)

DMC Coton Perlé No. 12, Red 666 (1 reel)

Tapestry needle size 24

Fine, sharp-pointed scissors

Few gold or silver beads (optional)

Beading needle and invisible thread if attaching beads

Spray starch

Instructions

1 Read and refer to the section on Hardanger techniques and stitches, pages 24-33. Prepare the linen as described. The fabric allowance is quite generous to make the small decorations easier to handle.

2 Following the chart and the key, work the buttonhole stitch outline starting at A, at a point 5cm (2in) in from two edges.

3 For the red tree, fill in the separate Kloster blocks, eyelets and diamond-shaped buttonhole stitches forming the pot for the tree. Withdraw the threads for the needleweaving and dove's eye filling.

4 Stitch the beads in place by slipping the beading needle through the back of the needleweaving.

5 Cut the embroidery away from the background fabric (page 32) and spray with starch to stiffen.

6 Attach a loop of thread at the top and your own choice of tassel at the bottom.

7 For the green tree, use DMC Coton Perlé No. 8, Green 699 and work the buttonhole outline stitch, filling in the pot for the tree as before. Do not cut and withdraw any threads.

8 Referring to the chart, work Kloster blocks instead of needleweaving.

9 Change to the DMC Coton Perlé No. 12, Red 666 and fill in all the Kloster block squares with eyelets.

10 Stitch beads, attach loop and tassel as above.

Alternative ideas and suggestions

- Change the colourways.
- Work a number of trees to make into a Christmas mobile.
- For a stiffer effect work on canvas (22 threads to the inch) sprayed with gold paint.

KEY

Use a single strand of DMC Coton Perlé throughout. Each grid line represents one line of fabric.

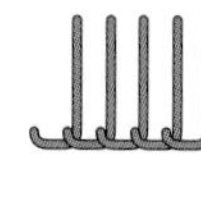

Red Tree
Buttonhole stitch edging
DMC Coton Perlé No. 8, Red 666

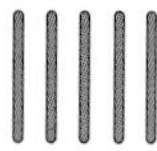

Kloster Blocks
DMC Coton Perlé No. 8, Red 666

Eyelets
DMC Coton Perlé No. 12, Red 666

Needleweaving & dove's eye filling
DMC Coton Perlé No. 12, Red 666

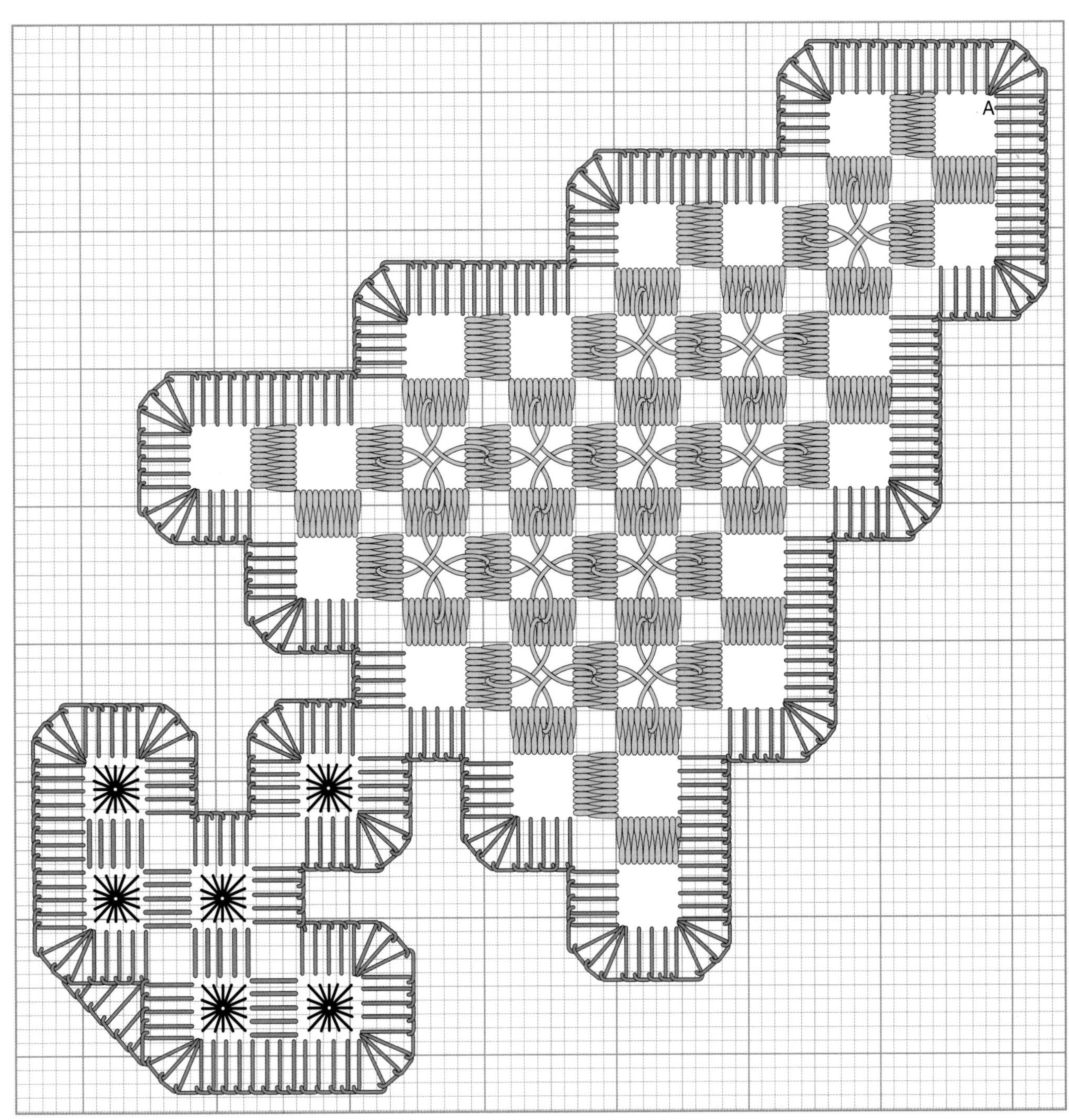
A

CONVERSION CHARTS

Crewel wool (yarn)

Appleton	Paternayan
353	604
354	602
355	601
428	620
438	680
447	841
465	540/571
503	950
744	503*
747	502*
749	500*
756	901*
824	540
835	660
852	572
871	716
872	714
941	907*
943	905*
945	904*
991b	260

* Closest match available.

Appleton and Paternayan yarns are available in skeins or hanks.

Stranded cotton (floss)

Anchor	DMC
1	White
46	3801
73	3689
118	341
119	3746
120	800
130	809
134	820
136	799
144	800
150	336
214	3814
228	910
235	317
259	772
260	369
261	368
262	3346
264	3348
265	3348
267	470
268	937
278	472
268	937
278	472
292	3078
293	727
295	726
300	745
392	642
852	822
883	3778
884	356
894	3688
1021	761
1041	844

List of Suppliers

UK

Appleton Brothers Ltd
Thames Works
Church Street
Chiswick
London W4 2PE
Tel: 0181 994 0711
Appleton wool

WHI Tapestry Shop Ltd
85 Pimlico Road
London SW1W 8PH
Tel: 0171 730 5366
Appleton wool (mail-order)

Spinning Jenny
Bradley
Keighley
West Yorkshire BD20 9DD
Tel: 0535 632469
Appleton wool (mail-order)

Shades at Mace and Nairn
89 Crane Street
Salisbury
Wiltshire SP1 2PY
Tel: 01722 336903
Appleton wool and embroidery specialists

Ginny's Heirlooms
56 Park House Gardens
Twickenham
Middlesex TW1 2DE
Tel: 0181 892 3246
Heirloom sewing, lace, fabrics and smocking supplies

Mulberry Silks
2 Old Rectory Cottage
Easton Grey
Malmsebury
Wiltshire SN16 0PE
Tel: 01666 840881
Myriad selection of silk threads

Ribbon Designs
42 Lake View
Edgware
Middlesex HA8 7RU
Tel: 0181 958 4966
Mail-order service for ribbons, including full range of pure silk ribbons and ribbons for embroidery.

Village Fabrics (retail shop)
Upstairs at Unit 7
Bushells Business Estate
Hithercroft
Lester Way
Wallingford
Oxfordshire OX10 9DF

Village Fabrics (mail-order)
PO Box 43
Wallingford
Oxfordshire OX10 9DF
Tel: 01491 836178
Patchwork and quilting supplies, specialising in 100% cotton American fabrics, books and haberdashery for quilters.

The Cheap Shop
108 Church Road
Tiptree
Essex
Tel: 01621 815576
American patchwork prints, books, haberdashery department, embroidery and craft items, beads, fabric and stencil paints.

DMC Creative World PLC
Pullman Road
Wigston
Leicester LE8 2DY
Tel: 0116 281 1040
(Fax 0116 281 3592)
Embroidery supplies, threads, linen

George Weil and Sons Limited
The Warehouse
Reading Arch Road
Redhill
Surrey RH1 1HG
Tel: 01737 778868 (Fax: 01737 778894)
All types of paints and fabrics for fabric painting

John Lewis
Oxford Street
London
Tel: 0171 629 7711
Extensive haberdashery department, large selection of cushion pads, including bolster and heart shape

Stef Francis
Waverley
Higher Rocombe
Stokeinteignhead
Newton Abbot
Devon TQ12 4QL
Tel and Fax: 01803 323004
Space dyed threads and fabrics

The Bead Merchant
38 Eld Lane
Colchester
Essex C01 1LS
Tel: 01206 764101 (Fax: 01206 76402)
Beads, (including Delica beads) semi precious stones and courses in beadwork

The Bead Shop
43 Neal Street
London WC2H 9PJ
Tel: 0171 240 0931
All types of beads

Sarah Deem
16 Hungerford Road
Lower Weston
Bath
Somerset BA1 3BU
Tel: 01225 339294
Exclusive hand-made traditional christening wear

Clive Beardall,
104b High Street
Maldon
Essex CM9 7ET
Tel: 01621 867890
Craftsman specialising in furniture restoration, marquetry, carving, decorative finishes and furniture made to order, including small boxes.

Coats Crafts UK
PO Box 22
The Lingfield Estate
Mc Mullen Road
Darlington
Co. Durham DL1 1YQ
Consumer Services Helpline:
Tel: 01325 365457
Embroidery supplies, Anchor threads, linen

CMP Habico Limited
Units B4-5
Wellington Road
Industrial Estate
Leeds
West Yorkshire LS12 2UA
Tel: 0113 244 9810
Fax 0113 242 5077
Haberdashery supplies including Mettler thread

Lowery Workstands
Bentley Lane
Grasby
Barnetby
South Humberside
DN38 6AW
Tel: 01652 628240
Steel workstands for embroidery and patchwork

USA

Kasuri Dye Works
1959 Shattuck Avenue
Berkeley CA 94704
Tel: (519) 841 4509
Japanese fabrics sashiko threads, needles, acetate patterns, thimbles.

Lydia's
900 Bogwallace Avenue
No. 104 Huntsville
Alabama 35801
Tel: (205) 536 9700
Heirloom sewing supplies

Martha Pullen
581 Madison Street
Huntsville
Alabama 35801
Tel: (205) 533 9586
Heirloom sewing supplies and courses

Carolyn Hook
It's a Crewel World
127 Essex Street
Salem
MA 01970-3706
Tel: (508) 745 9696
Suppliers of DMC, Paternayan, silk threads, Zweigart and other imported canvas, fabric and books

INDEX